RICHARD WAGNER

Hans Gal

RICHARD WAGNER

————————

Translated by
Hans-Hubert Schönzeler

LONDON
VICTOR GOLLANCZ LTD
1976

© Fischer Bücherei KG, Frankfurt am Main, 1963
English translation © Victor Gollancz Ltd, 1976

ISBN 0 575 01847 x

Printed in Great Britain by
The Camelot Press Ltd, Southampton

CONTENTS

TRANSLATOR'S NOTE

Reputedly Alfred Cortot once said: "There are two ways of interpreting music: with respect—or by violating it. Unfortunately the former leads nowhere. That is why I have chosen the latter." In the same sense I have violated Hans Gal.

Hans Gal's German has a style very much of its own, which lends all his writings a peculiar attraction and fascination. Even in translation this has to be preserved in order to project the unique personality which lies behind his words—but any strict, literal translation would defeat this object. I have therefore tried to render the spirit of Hans Gal in English rather than his actual words, and I shall consider myself happy if I have succeeded to some extent.

The quotations from Wagner's letters and writings presented a similar problem. As is well known, Wagner's style is flowery and contorted in the extreme. I have not drawn on existing translations, most of which are somewhat tortuous—instead, I have tried to give a readable English equivalent of what Wagner *meant* to say rather than an academic word-by-word translation of his texts. Similarly, when Gal quotes from the opera texts to give samples of Wagner's propensities as a "poet", I have preferred to translate such excerpts freely in order to stress his points (cf. p. 156). Should I have violated the susceptibilities of the purist, may the Lord have mercy on me!

LONDON,
FEBRUARY 1975

HANS-HUBERT SCHÖNZELER

INTRODUCTION

Von der Parteien Gunst und Hass verwirrt,
Schwankt sein Charakterbild in der Geschichte.
                                    SCHILLER

"Blurred by the favour and hate of parties,
his image wavers in our history."
                            (transl. C. E. Passage)

NO OTHER ARTIST has ever kept the public at large in such
a state of suspense as did Richard Wagner. Even decades after
his death the battle of public opinion for and against him and
his work continued to rage with unabated fury, and one could
fill a library with the books dealing with those pros and cons.
The number of biographies and monographs is virtually
uncountable, and there is hardly one important or unimportant
event in his life which has not been investigated and amply
documented. All his letters, as far as they could be unearthed,
have been published, and in addition Wagner himself took
good care that there should be sufficient autobiographical
material. This begins with a sketch from the time of *Rienzi*
(Dresden, 1842) up to his comprehensive memoirs *Mein Leben*
("My Life", 1870) which unfortunately ends with the fateful
and decisive year 1864. Despite the fact that it gives no information about the last nineteen years of Wagner's life, it is nevertheless one of the most valuable sources as regards his development,
his inner as well as his external life. Of course, it cannot be
denied that this literary work was supervised by a strict censor:
Wagner dictated it to Cosima von Bülow, with whom he had
intimate relations at that time, and who shortly afterwards
became his wife. So he had to be considerate to this secretary
and veil and suppress many a fact, such as for instance the

details of the Wesendonck affair in Zürich. Cosima, daughter of Liszt, twenty-four years younger than Wagner (whom she outlived by many years), gifted, ambitious, energetic, had only one aim, which she pursued with an amazing singularity of purpose: ever to increase the greatness and glory of her late husband. Without scruples or inhibitions she sifted the material, and whatever did not appear to her to fit into the image which she was building up, no matter for what reason, simply "vanished". But to this day Wahnfried, the Bayreuth villa of the Wagner family, must still contain quite a few diaries and letters which have been carefully concealed from the eyes of the public—if they have not been destroyed long ago. The Burrell Collection, published in 1950, has added much to our knowledge in this respect, in particular as regards some hitherto unknown letters from Wagner to his first wife Minna.

Karl Friedrich Glasenapp's six-volume biography of Richard Wagner is officially sanctioned by Wahnfried. Glasenapp treats his subject with the fussy and pedantic verbosity of a German professor, but at the same time he is also perfectly happy to suppress, distort and gloss over any inconvenient facts with a dexterity which otherwise can only be found in extreme cases in the sycophantic writings of court biographers and court historians. With his comprehensive four-volume biography Ernest Newman undertook the enormous task of rectifying the most important points and filling many gaps, which has greatly increased our knowledge of Wagner, particularly of the years in Munich, Triebschen and Bayreuth.

Both as a personality and as an artist Wagner poses a problem of the most fantastic contradictions, and every estimation of his character must of necessity be out of kilter unless it is based on profound understanding of the tremendous scale of his achievement. But only nowadays, over the span of virtually a century, is it possible to judge his artistic defects, an assessment which must be based on a broad overall view and not belittling the positive elements of his work. This book is an attempt, in brief and terse terms, to come to grips with the man and the artist, with his problems, his contradictions, his absurdities, in as objective a manner as possible. For many a long year Wagner has been a god for some, an object of revulsion for others. There are valid reasons for both attitudes, but the real truth lies much deeper and is much more complicated than may appear to the superficial or prejudiced beholder.

PART I

THE LIFE OF AN ADVENTURER

CHILDHOOD AND YOUTH
(1813–1839)

TO CALL WAGNER an adventurer is not necessarily a sacrilege, if we consider as an adventurer a person who has a constitutional tendency to fantastic decisions, to actions and omissions the results of which are unpredictable and which presuppose an uninhibited and boundless optimism. These are tendencies which dominated Wagner's entire life. Again and again they led him into tight corners, into inner as well as outer conflicts. Warrants were issued for his arrest, he spent years in exile, had many erotic entanglements, lived in continual fear of the debtors' prison—yet in the end those tendencies also led him to an apotheosis, a triumph such as no other artist before him had ever experienced.

Wilhelm Richard Wagner was born in Leipzig on 22 May 1813. His father Friedrich Wagner, a police actuary, died shortly afterwards, and in August of the following year his widow, Johanna Wagner, married the actor Ludwig Geyer, a member of the Leipzig theatre ensemble, who had been an intimate friend of the family for some time. The first child of this second marriage, Cäcilie, was born six months later. Richard appears to have been the favourite of his step-father, and he always held Geyer (who died in 1821) in great affection. A portrait of Geyer hung on the walls of the Bayreuth study, and Glasenapp reports that on one occasion Wagner commented on the fact that there seemed to be a strange resemblance between this portrait and his little son Siegfried. This seems to indicate that he himself must have had certain suspicions regarding his origin—suspicions which are not too far-fetched, and which are further strengthened by a fact of which Wagner can hardly have known: contemporary records have proved that on 21 July 1813 Johanna Wagner (undoubtedly with her two-month-old baby) was in Teplitz in the same inn as Geyer, who was there on tour with the Leipzig ensemble. That she undertook this journey a matter of three months before the Battle of Leipzig, at a time of extreme unrest and under difficult and even dangerous conditions, gives more than food for thought. Little is known about Friedrich Wagner, but Geyer was a man of many talents: apart from his activity in the theatre he also had some success as a dramatic author and a portrait painter. To the seven Wagner children he was always a good and solicitous father. Incidentally, there is no documentary proof whatsoever for Nietzsche's surmise that Geyer was of Jewish origin.

In 1814 the family moved to Dresden, where Geyer had become a member of the *Hoftheater*. In the circumstances it is obvious that the children, as they grew up, were constantly in touch with the theatrical world, and several of Wagner's brothers and sisters took up a stage career. After Geyer's premature death Richard's eldest sister Rosalie, who was an actress at the Dresden *Hoftheater*, became the financial mainstay of the indigent family; for the rest they were dependent on assistance from relatives and the modest income which they could earn by letting out rooms. From the age of eight Richard had to grow up without any paternal authority, and this unavoidably had an unfavourable influence on the early years of his development. According to his own account he must have been a difficult child. First in Dresden, and later during his high-school days in Leipzig—and always more or less as a little revolutionary against the scholastic authorities—the boy threatened to drift into the paths of a dramatic author. As a natural consequence of his early contact with the theatre, he terrified his entire family by producing, at the mere age of fifteen, *Leubold und Adelaide*, a romantic drama in the best blood-and-thunder tradition. At around that time he also began to take an interest in music—not so much on account of his own little efforts as a pianist, but much more through the inspiring experiences he received from listening to Beethoven's symphonies and to operas. *Der Freischütz* in particular made an indelible impression on him, especially as Weber, then *Hofkapellmeister* in Dresden, was on a very friendly footing with the Geyer family. Nevertheless, Wagner was nearing his eighteenth birthday when, under the guidance of *Thomaskantor* Weinlig, he first began a serious study of harmony and counterpoint, and he says himself that these studies were of such thoroughness as to furnish him with an excellent basis for his future composi-tional technique. What he composed during those years—a piano sonata, several overtures, a symphony—gives evidence of sound training, nothing else. Wagner was no infant prodigy, nor is there much more indication of the "future genius" in the opera *Die Feen* which he began in his twentieth year (based on Gozzi's *La donna serpente*) and which dutifully follows in the rut of German romantic opera with all its reminiscences of Beethoven, Weber and Marschner.

An attempt to get *Die Feen* accepted for performance in Leipzig came to nought, but meanwhile the young Wagner had gained his first practical experience at the theatre in Würzburg where his brother Albert was one of the tenors. In autumn 1834 Wagner proceeded to the Magdeburg theatre as *Musikdirektor*—chorus master and second conductor—and here he had his first successes as a conductor. In the following season he was promoted to First Conductor and also completed the composition of a new opera, *Das Liebesverbot* (based on Shakespeare's *Measure for Measure*), of which he gave one single performance in March 1836. Immediately afterwards the theatre had to declare bankrupt and close down. The most important acquisitions of his time in Magdeburg were debts, which had accumulated in the main as the result of a concert which he had put on himself with expensive artists—and Minna Planer, the prettiest and most successful actress of the company, with whom Wagner had a tender *liaison*. In November of that year 1836 she became his wife in Königsberg, where they had both found new posts.

Minna was the first true passion of the young Wagner. He was tempestuously in love, but she was the carefully reticent partner of this thoughtlessly concluded marriage. Being four years his senior, she had more experience in life and a reflective coolness, and although she admired and adored the fiery young artist, she obviously had no understanding at all for the higher, more esoteric ends of his ambitions. She herself could hardly be termed truly musical, and probably her own artistic activity (which, incidentally, she gave up soon after her marriage) did not mean more to her than a means of earning her living. In Magdeburg the love affair between Richard and Minna was a dramatic chain of episodes and crises; wedded bliss proceeded much along the same lines from the very beginning. Wagner, like a *prima donna*, was despotic and as jealous as the devil. Half a year after their marriage Minna fled back to her parents in Dresden, because she could not stand the strain of life with Wagner. He dropped everything and followed her, and after many endeavours on his part—endeavours which took up the whole of that summer—he succeeded in smoothing out those sources of friction which had nearly resulted in a divorce.

Conditions at the theatre in Königsberg were not particularly edifying. Wagner had incurred another lot of debts, which meant yet another embarrassment, and so he decided to accept an offer to come to Riga as *Kapellmeister* where, under the direction of Karl von Holtei (who later acquired a certain measure of fame as a poet and writer), a new theatre had been founded under the Balto-German aegis of the citizenry of this Russian town. In his memoirs Wagner gives a graphic description of the conditions in German theatres at the beginning of his career. It is hard to imagine anything more primitive. The stages of towns such as Magdeburg or Königsberg were in the hands of a director, who managed them on his own financial responsibility with possibly some insignificant subsidies from this source or that, and provided both drama and opera. The personnel as a rule was underpaid and second-rate, chorus and orchestra abysmal, with the repertoire restricted to such works as promoted box-office and were inexpensive as regards scenery requirements. The nucleus of the operatic repertoire comprised the successful French and Italian operas by composers such as Bellini, Donizetti, Auber, Hérold, Adam; the main source of the evil was, however, the insecurity of the financial set-up. When Wagner took up his post at the Magdeburg theatre he wrote: "I was warned that, if I was really set on getting the salary due to me, I would only do so by making myself pleasant to Mme. Bethmann [wife of the director]." In Königsberg matters were no better. Towards the end of the season the director had to appeal "to the devoted assistance of the personnel, in order to secure the continued existence of the theatre". Shortly afterwards, of course, Minna and Richard Wagner took French leave of Königsberg and thereby saved themselves the trouble of having to give their "devoted assistance".

Apparently conditions in Riga were more favourable initially, as the town had managed to raise a sizeable fund to support its theatre. Wagner, who by now had the routine and the repertoire of the common-or-garden opera *Kapellmeister*, had a reasonably efficient ensemble at his disposal and occasionally managed to produce performances which gave even him some measure of satisfaction. But he was sick to death of provincial conditions and now, in grandiose manner, he planned a monumental work in the style of French *grand opéra*. It was the time when Meyerbeer was reaping sensational successes with *Robert le Diable* and *Les Huguenots*, and it was in the wake of these great historical panoramas that Wagner conceived his *Rienzi*. Bulwer-Lytton had just published a novel under this title, and in an incredibly short time Wagner adapted and suited the text to his purpose. During the second winter of his Riga period (1838–39) he composed the music of the first two acts. From Magdeburg he had written to the famous French librettist Eugène Scribe, suggesting some form of collaboration—a letter which, needless to say, remained unanswered. Now he writes to the almighty Meyerbeer, begging for recommendation and patronage. Even at this early age Wagner is a virtuoso letter writer: he knows precisely what he wants and how to press his case with conviction. *En face* Meyerbeer he really lays it on thick: he tells of the one-sidedness of his earliest beginnings, when he was completely influenced by Beethoven, and then continues:

Since then, and especially since I came into contact with the actual life and practical aspects of music, my views about present-day conceptions have altered drastically, above all as far as the dramatic side is concerned. Should I deny that it was particularly *your* works which have given me the pointer to a new direction? In any case it would not here be

fitting to indulge in uncouth flatteries as regards your genius.
May I just say that in your music I saw the perfect solution
of the true German, who absorbed the best aspects of the
Italian and French schools in order to give the creations of
his mind a universal import.

The thought of Paris kept him in a permanent state of unrest,
that Paris where Gluck, Spontini, Meyerbeer, Bellini had made
their rise to world fame. In Riga—this just happened to be his
character—he made a few more debts. Meanwhile his old
creditors in Magdeburg and Königsberg were getting impatient
too and instigated legal proceedings. So when it turned out
that his contract, which ended with the current season, would
not be renewed, he decided to do a moonlight flit.

Unfortunately he was short of funds, even to this end, but
luckily a devoted friend from Königsberg who happened to
visit him at the time could provide assistance and help. As
secretly as possible all assets were turned into ready cash,
especially the furniture—which had been bought in Königsberg
on borrowed money anyway. The fact that neither Scribe nor
Meyerbeer had replied to his letters did not disconcert Wagner
in the least.

To me, on the other hand, it was quite sufficient to be able
to say that I was in contact with Paris. When I tackled this
daring enterprise of mine from Riga, I truly imagined
that I had a solid point of contact and, as far as my Paris
plans were concerned, was not really building castles in
Spain.

The Königsberg friend Abraham Möller put his carriage at
Wagner's disposal to help him reach an East Prussian port via
the Russian border:

Somehow or other we had to manage to cross this border
without passports, as ours had been confiscated by various
creditors. . . . I was so desirous to get away from my present
situation at any price and, as soon as possible, to reach those
great prospects from which I was expecting the satisfaction

of all my ambitions that I was blind to the adversities which inevitably had to accompany the execution of my recent decisions.

In all secrecy they crossed the border by night under constant danger of being discovered and arrested by cossacks on patrol; and then followed a tedious journey, lasting several days, in uncomfortable local carts. By-passing Königsberg—where they could not allow themselves to be seen—they travelled over bad roads to the small port of Pillau, where they boarded a London-bound sailing-ship:

As the captain had to accept us aboard without passports, this again presented a new difficulty. Before daybreak we had to make our secret way in a small boat past the harbour guards and try to sneak on board. Once we had got there, and after with great difficulty we had managed to get Robber [a huge Newfoundland dog whom Wagner refused to leave behind] up the steep ship's side without attracting attention, we immediately had to hide on one of the lower decks in order to escape the notice of any last visitor before the ship's departure. Finally anchor was weighed, and as by and by the shore slipped out of sight we thought that now we could breathe a sigh of relief and recover our composure.

2

YEARS OF DEARTH
(1839–1842)

WITH HIS FLIGHT to Paris, with this utterly fantastic prelude to an adventure, Wagner entered a new period of his life. It was a period full of suffering, but at the same time of the most decisive significance, as it was then that his true genius emerged unmistakably. The flight itself is a model for similar actions in times of crisis which are to form part of the pattern for the rest of his life. Again and again they are caused by a chain of internal and external circumstances which eventually reach an insupportable level, and his desire to achieve an escape becomes such an obsession that no sacrifice seems too great, no danger too threatening. First of all there are those perennial debts. As he is incapable of denying himself anything which at the moment he may consider necessary or desirable, he cheerfully goes on borrowing money whilst there is still someone willing to lend it to him—and his burning ambition, his uninhibited dreams never allow him to be contented with what actually lies within his reach. The result? Feelings of listlessness, those unavoidable frictions (inherent in all practical activities) with the world around him and its contradictory interests, and added to that the everlasting threat of bailiff and debtors' prison. All this together eventually reaches a point where his rational judgment ceases to function and he gives in to the enticement of phantasmagoric visions. The sanguine optimist grasps at straws and is happily prepared to consider every castle in the air as a reality.

In 1839 a voyage from Riga to Paris was an undertaking in comparison with which a trip around the world in our day and age is child's play:

We were on board a trader of the smallest type. She was

called *Thetis*, bore the figure head of that nymph on her poop and, including the captain, had a crew of seven. Everyone was of the opinion that in fine weather, such as one thought one could expect in summer, the crossing to London would take eight days. But even at the outset, in the Baltic, we were becalmed and held up for a long time. . . . After seven days' sailing we had only reached Copenhagen where, without leaving the ship, we took the opportunity of making our very sparse ship's diet somewhat more bearable by buying some additional food and drink. . . . So, full of hope, we sailed through the Kattegat towards the Skagerrak where the wind, which initially had been merely unfavourable and forced us to tack laboriously, reached gale force proportions on the second day of this new journey. For a full twenty-four hours we had to battle against sufferings which were completely new to us. Cooped up in the miserable captain's cabin, without a proper bedstead for either of us, we were at the mercy of seasickness and terrors. . . . Finally, on 27 July, the westerly gale forced the captain to seek the shelter of a port on the Norwegian coast. With a feeling of relief I looked out on the long stretched-out rocky shore. We approached at great speed, and after a Norwegian pilot, who had come to meet us in his small boat, had taken the helm of the *Thetis* into his skilful hands, I soon experienced one of the most wonderful and beautiful impressions of my life. What I had taken for a continuous rocky shore line, as we approached it turned out to be a chain of single cone-shaped rocks jutting out from the sea. When we had passed them we could perceive that we were now surrounded by these reefs, not only in front of us and at either side, but also behind us, where they were so close together that they appeared to form one single stretch of rock. At the same time these rocks in our rear broke the force of the gale, and as our voyage proceeded further through this ever-changing labyrinth of cone-shaped rocks, the sea became gradually calmer. At long last, entering one of those long water-ways through a rocky valley (this was how a Norwegian fjord presented itself to me) the ship sailed along perfectly smoothly and peacefully. A feeling of well-being came over me when the shouts of our crew re-echoed from the enormous walls of granite: they dropped anchor and furled the sails. The brief rhythm of their shouts remained in my ears like a consoling premonition and eventually took its final shape in the theme of the sailors' chorus in my "Flying Dutchman"—for which the basic idea was even then in my head and which, under the impressions which I had just experienced, gained a definitive musico-poetical timbre.

After two days of rest they continued their journey. Because of a minor incident it was interrupted once more, and then they went on again:

After four days we had a northerly wind which brought us ahead very quickly in the right direction. Already we thought that soon we should be at the end of our journey, when on the evening of 6 August the favourable wind changed and a storm of incredible fury blew up. It was not merely the terrible force with which the ship was tossed up and down without direction, a playball of the monstrous ocean, presenting itself to me now as the lowest abyss, now as the sheer peak of a mountain, which produced a shudder of death within me— it was rather the waning courage of the crew: I noticed their despairing and malicious looks; superstitiously they seemed to consider us the cause of their impending shipwreck. They did not know of the trifling reasons for the secrecy of our journey and may easily have thought that our enforced flight might have a dubious, possibly criminal background. At the height of this peril even the captain seemed to regret ever having taken us on board, as apparently we had brought him misfortune on this occasion—he had so often done this journey, particularly in summer, in a short time and without any difficulty.

For days the ship battled its way through the storms and finally sailed up the Thames, where it docked on 12 August. Three-and-a-half weeks they had been at sea. At the beginning of the journey the Wagners had 100 ducats to call their own— funds which resulted from realizing their assets in Riga.

Expenses during the journey had already reduced this sum. Now, after the strain of the crossing, they had to recuperate in London, and the money melted in their hands. When they finally reached Boulogne on 20 August, it was "not without certain fears and premonition of disappointments".

Nevertheless, it was a pleasant surprise to hear that Meyerbeer—Patron Saint of the entire expedition without his consent ever having been asked!—happened to be in Boulogne at the time. Of course Wagner made the most of this fortuitous circumstance and immediately paid his respects to Meyerbeer, who accorded his young fellow-countryman a cordial reception and showed definite interest in the *Rienzi* score, of which Wagner could show him two acts (the other three had not yet been composed). To jump ahead and anticipate the end of a long-drawn-out and rather piteous business: Meyerbeer was the only person who did something positive for that young musician, stranded in foreign parts, and who gave him some effective assistance in those first and most arduous moments of his career.

As a first step he gave him a letter of recommendation to the director of the *Opéra* and to Habeneck, its principal conductor. Towards the middle of September our travellers reached Paris, which impressed them as being narrow, dirty and depressing. Avenarius, who was about to marry Wagner's youngest sister Cäcilie and thus become his brother-in-law, lived in Paris and had fixed simple quarters for them, but it seems that very soon he developed some measure of scepticism towards these relatives who were ever in need of money, and he kept his pockets buttoned up. The various notabilities to whom Wagner had been recommended also withdrew discreetly, offering no more than polite phrases. The only practical result was that Habeneck invited him to attend the rehearsals of the excellent Conservatoire Orchestra: here he could hear Beethoven symphonies, amongst them the Ninth, in first-rate performances, and they gave his *Columbus* Overture a play-through—a piece which he had composed in Magdeburg for a drama by the Leipzig friend of his youth, Theodor Apel. Also as a result of Meyerbeer's recommendation, *Das Liebesverbot* was accepted for performance at the *Théâtre de la Renaissance*, but this acceptance can hardly have been meant very seriously, as soon afterwards the theatre had to declare bankrupt. Wagner was in a desperate position. Everything which had the slightest value went to the pawnbrokers. Incidentally, since the Königsberg and Riga days the Wagner *ménage* had also comprised Minna's supposed sister Natalie; in actual fact she was her daughter, the result of a little lapse when Minna was fifteen, but Wagner only learnt the truth about that many years later. Robber, the huge Newfoundland dog, has already been mentioned, and to keep him fed was a major problem in Paris. One day he ran away and was seen no more.

With the intention of writing something which would find an easy market, Wagner composed a number of French Romances, but he found no takers. One of them, a setting of Heine's *Die beiden Grenadiere* in a French translation, Wagner had printed at his own expense, but he still achieved no sales. First Schlesinger—a publisher to whom Meyerbeer had also recommended him—had to bear the costs of this transaction, and as a compensation Wagner wrote an article for the *Gazette Musicale*, a musical journal which Schlesinger issued. Wagner's article aroused some interest, so that in future this journal gave him a modest source of income, and Schlesinger was quite prepared to offer the indigent musician a few bits and pieces of editorial work which kept the wolf from the door for some time: vocal scores of operas, arrangements for all sorts of instruments and many things of this sort—including a *Méthode pour Cornet à Pistons*, a paste-and-scissors effort resulting in fourteen medleys on popular operatic airs.

Slowly, during this sorrowful first year in Paris, the *Rienzi* score had reached completion. As there was no chance of the *Opéra* accepting it, Wagner had the idea of writing a one-act "opening" opera such as was occasionally performed in Paris before an evening of ballet. To this end he made a first draft for *Der fliegende Holländer* ("The Flying Dutchman")—the subject which, as mentioned earlier, had attracted his imagination for some time. Now Meyerbeer, who had been abroad for a while, introduced Wagner to the new director of the *Opéra*, Léon Pillet. Pillet saw the draft libretto and was interested, but the consequence was perhaps the greatest humiliation to which

Wagner was ever subjected in Paris, for Pillet suggested that he would acquire it in order to have it set to music by one of the composers to whom he was contractually tied. "There was no possibility whatsoever within the next seven years of commisioning any composition from me, not even a short opera, as the commitments which the director had entered upon were sufficient for that period." So Wagner left *Le Vaisseau Fantôme* to its fate for a paltry 500 francs—but with that money he could buy himself the time to complete the music for *Der fliegende Holländer*. As a matter of interest, *Le Vaisseau Fantôme* was actually set to music by one Pierre Louis Philippe Dietsch, a French composer of German origin; it was staged and then died a peaceful death. Later in life Wagner and Dietsch came into personal contact, of which more anon. . . .

It is not easy to imagine the emotions of an ambitious young artist who feels within himself the ferment of productive forces and unbelievable tensions, who is only waiting for the opportunity of showing what he can do, who knocks on door after door and finds them all barred and bolted, who has to eke out his living by what amounts to menial tasks. That resplendent Paris of the days of Louis Philippe, that Paris of Victor Hugo, Balzac, Dumas, Chopin, Heine, Liszt, Berlioz (the two last-named he even met briefly), that Paris bubbling over with *joie de vivre*—to Wagner it was nothing but a desert of brick and mortar, his existence nothing but the problem of procuring the daily bread. Minna was ever kind and patient. She was a devoted companion, and he could not have found a better one, even though those days remained a nightmare in her memories. Ten years later she wrote to Wagner: "You must not take it amiss if I am worried about our day-to-day existence: I simply cannot repeat the experiences through which once before I suffered with you. When I remember those petty worries about our food, when sometimes I did not know what to put into the boiling water because I didn't have anything, then indeed the thought of my future terrifies me, because a similar state of affairs seems to lie ahead of me. . . ." Meanwhile a small circle of compatriots had gathered around the Wagners: the painter Kietz, the philologist Lehrs, the librarian Anders. Poor devils, all of them, and they helped each other as best they could—that is to say, they shared their last franc with Wagner. One of his letters (3 June 1840) to Kietz is more than eloquent: "I have had news today and now know that I will not have any more money for another fortnight or three weeks . . . I beg you, don't turn down the request of an anguished friend and, if you have any money, for Heaven's sake let your tailor wait for those two or three weeks and help me until then. . . ." It is true that Wagner's own tailor had to wait just as much: even in his Dresden days, when he was a well-salaried *Hofkapellmeister*, he still had a long correspondence with Kietz about that bill of his Paris tailor, until he finally decided to settle up—at the expense of the Dresden *prima donna* Schröder-Devrient from whom he borrowed the necessary.

It is understandable that Wagner, in his memoirs, was somewhat reticent about mentioning an episode which, in that fateful year 1840, was the true nadir of his misery: there is documentary evidence that at the end of October he really landed in the debtors' prison. Minna wrote to Wagner's Leipzig friend Theo Apel who had pulled him out of the mire on earlier occasions:

A few words will suffice to tell you the reason for this letter: this morning Richard has had to leave me in order to take up his quarters in the debtors' prison. I am still terribly upset and everything seems to be swimming in front of my eyes. . . . I was terrified when, on an earlier occasion, I discovered how much Richard owes you already. At that time on the strength of your credit you obtained funds for him, but what was his situation then in comparison to the present one? Such a sacrifice would be infinitely better applied now, if only because there is the prospect that such a debt could surely be repaid within the course of one year, two at the most.

This is the very voice of Wagner himself, whose draft of this letter has been preserved. A few weeks later he was in the same old dilemma and wrote to another friend of his younger days, Heinrich Laube, on 3 December 1840:

No one can ever live through days more horrible than the first and second of this unfortunate month have been for me. As far as was possible, the last few pence of my poor friends here have helped me to avert the fateful blow up to the 15th of the month—but this blow will irrevocably mean the immediate seizure of all my property and loss of my personal freedom. . . . I am now endeavouring, by hook or by crook, to raise the requisite funds; should you be able to contribute something—be it what it may—please send it immediately!

Such worries and the continued hack work for Schlesinger took up the spring of 1841. Early in July he sold the *Holländer* idea to the *Opéra* and the receipt of those 500 francs produced a miracle such as happened again and again throughout Wagner's life: in a trance of creative frenzy, within the short span of seven weeks, he composed the music of this opera, the text of which he had presumably begun in prison and completed during his few hours of leisure in the course of that winter. The *Holländer* may lack maturity, but as a work of genius it is second to none of his later creations. In the whole history of music there is hardly another instance comparable to this sudden break-through of a talented beginner into the realms of true genius. Wagner himself bathed in the glory of his creative potency:

I can only report one thing: after this short and yet so intense period during which I could follow the call of my innermost self, dedicating myself to the consolation of pure artistic creation, I had reached a point which enabled me to look forward to a prolonged period of disturbance and adversity with much more equanimity. It came with greatest punctuality: just as I had reached the end of the final scene, my 500 francs were exhausted: they did not last long enough to secure the necessary peace of mind for me to compose the overture. I had to defer this until there should be a new favourable change in my situation and now, battling under conditions of all sorts which were robbing me of time and equanimity, I had once again to fight for my bare existence.

When the next impasse was reached, the good Kietz again found an uncle who could advance some money. "With a sort of pride I often showed him my boots at that time, for in the end they really were no more than an illusory kind of footwear, the soles finally having disintegrated completely."

At last, by November, the Overture was completed. By submitting the text of the opera, Wagner tried to raise interest for his *Holländer* in Leipzig as well as in Munich, but without success. In Leipzig they found the theme too sombre, and Munich thought that the work did not conform to the taste of German audiences. Now he sent the score to Meyerbeer in Berlin who, as *Generalmusikdirektor*, would soon have unlimited power there. Much earlier Wagner (using Meyerbeer's name as a recommendation) had submitted *Rienzi* to the *Hoftheater* in Dresden, and from both sides he received favourable news: *Der fliegende Holländer* was accepted for performance in Berlin, *Rienzi* in Dresden. By the time Wagner wrote his memoirs, Meyerbeer had already become the favourite butt of his hatred, and he tried as well as he could to belittle Meyerbeer's share in these early successes. However, the archives of the theatres of Berlin and Dresden leave no room for doubt that Meyerbeer promoted the cause of his protégé to the best of his ability. Such a recommendation from the most famous opera composer of his day was of decisive importance and, as is evident from letters of that time, Wagner then acknowledged that fact fully and boasted with pride of the friendship which Meyerbeer extended to him.

So by the beginning of 1842 Wagner had got over the worst. Long ago he had realized that Paris was not the suitable soil for his talent, but with the prospect of performances of his works in Germany he now had a cogent reason for returning to his home country. The only trouble was: he needed money. First he tried his Dresden friends, whom he bombarded with letters asking them to push the *Rienzi* performance: originally it had been planned for February, but circumstances intervened, and the *première* had to be postponed and postponed. Finally he decided to take matters in hand himself—and now, as a result of his tangible prospects in Dresden, his moneyed relatives at long last did something for him: his brothers-in-law Avenarius and Friedrich Brockhaus provided him with the necessary funds for the journey. After seven days in the stage coach he and Minna reached Dresden on 12 April 1842, and immediately he went to see the General Director von Lüttichau and the conductor Reissiger at the theatre. As a rule people in the theatrical world are not particularly pleased at the arrival of a composer long before the first performance of one of his works, but nevertheless Wagner was well received. He encountered kindly persons who were well disposed towards him, amongst them the actor Ferdinand Heine (who in the old days had been a friend of Geyer's), the secretary of the theatre *Hofrat* Winkler and the chorus master Fischer, with whom he had corresponded from Paris. Apart from that the tenor Joseph Tichatschek, who had been engaged for the part of Rienzi and whom Wagner held in high estimation because of his vocal and musical excellence, was in any case prejudiced in favour of the opera, as he was to appear in most magnificent costumes. Despite all this the performance could not be billed for earlier than the autumn, which meant that for another six months the Wagners had to live on borrowed money.

Wagner's presence had one advantage: having had so much practical experience in the operatic world (a fact which immediately became apparent), he could give a creative impulse to the preparation of his own work. Fischer was worried about the enormous duration of the opera and suggested cuts:

He was quite honest about this, and I was perfectly happy to undertake this arduous task together with him. On an old grand piano in a rehearsal room of the *Hoftheater* I played and sang my score with such resounding energy to this flabbergasted fellow that he was quite willing to acquiesce to the loss of his piano and was only worried about my lungs. Under much laughter he gave up all argument about cuts— for especially in such places where he thought a cut might be possible, my overpowering eloquence proved to him that just this was essential. Head over heels together with me he submerged himself in the wallowing sound, and the only thing he could produce in justification of his own opinions was his pocket watch—but after a certain amount of disputation I defeated even this argument.

Wagner's fertile brain was never at rest. A walking holiday in the Bohemian Erzgebirge allowed the Tannhäuser idea to come to maturity. Again it was a subject which had fascinated him in Paris. By the end of July he was back in Dresden, rehearsing. Next to Tichatschek it was Schröder-Devrient (as Adriano) who gave Wagner the greatest artistic satisfaction. As a young man Wagner had had some of his greatest opera experiences from her interpretations, especially as Leonore in Beethoven's *Fidelio*, and throughout his years in Dresden she remained one of his staunch supporters. Wagner himself tells of the increasing interest with which the personnel of the *Hoftheater* took to the new work, and even the otherwise indolent *Kapellmeister* Reissiger gave more and more support. 20 October 1842 was the day of the *première*:

> Never again have I had similar emotions, not even by comparison, to those with which I attended the first performance of *Rienzi*. Well-founded worry for their success has always dominated my mind in all later first performances of my works to such an extent that I have never again been able to achieve any proper enjoyment of the work or even of the recognition on the part of the public. . . . Together with Minna, my sister Klara and the Heine family I was in a stalls box, and if I want to recall my own condition during this evening, I can only describe it as trance-like . . . I never noticed the applause, and when at the end of each act I was called out, my friend Heine always had to wake me forcibly out of my dream-world and push me on to the stage.

Fischer had been quite right: the performance lasted from 6 p.m. until midnight. But the public sat through it, and the evening was an unqualified triumph for the composer. Later some cuts were made, very much against the opposition of Tichatschek, who did not want to lose any of his plums. At times attempts were made to perform the opera in two sections on two successive evenings, but this proved unsuccessful as the public felt it was being cheated. *Rienzi* always had full houses and remained in the repertoire up to the time of the catastrophe which forced Wagner to leave Dresden seven years later.

3

HOFKAPELLMEISTER TO THE KING OF SAXONY

(1843–1849)

THAT PERFORMANCE OF *Rienzi*, Wagner's last "early" work, marks the beginning of another act in the drama of his life. With *Der fliegende Holländer* he achieved maturity in the world of music, and as a mature artist he now in Dresden entered on a period of most intense practical and creative activity. As a direct result of the *Rienzi* success he was offered the post of a *Hofkapellmeister* which had been vacant for some time. In this position he ranked equally with his colleague Reissiger, and suddenly he was rid of all material worries. That he was justifiably overjoyed at this turn in his affairs shines forth from a letter to his Paris friend Lehrs:

> I am being treated here with a distinction such as, under similar conditions, surely has never yet been accorded to anyone. Half a year ago I was a vagabond who would not have known how to obtain a passport—now I have a position for life with a good salary, with the prospect that this salary will continue to increase, and with a sphere of activity as only few have at their disposal. . . .

But of course it was not in Wagner's character to dedicate himself to this sphere of activity with all his heart, as Haydn did in Eisenstadt, Spohr in Kassel, Marschner in Hanover—and as poor Minna would have wished so very much.

For the moment he had reached the goal of his most ambitious dreams. No other opera composer has ever made his *début* under more favourable auspices. Granted, the production of *Der fliegende Holländer* in Berlin was delayed owing to a change in the administration: Graf Redern who had originally accepted the work left his post and was replaced by Herr von Küstner who, as *Intendant* in Munich, had rejected it. Wagner was suspicious of Meyerbeer as though the whole business had been a pre-arranged, put-up job, but he did him an injustice. In a letter of 5 December 1843 Meyerbeer, as *Generalmusikdirektor*, reminded the new *Intendant* that *Der fliegende Holländer* must be scheduled for performance in the near future, and that the cast had already been decided upon in consultation with the composer. But Dresden had beaten Berlin to it: after the sensational success of *Rienzi*, which remained in the repertoire as a box-office draw, the *Hoftheater* had immediately begun preparations for the *Holländer*, and the *première* took place on 2 January 1843.

Wagner was very unhappy with this performance; in artistic respects he was satisfied only with Schröder-Devrient's Senta, even though by then she was already somewhat matronly in appearance. What he did realize on this occasion was the tremendous importance of having the right cast for a first performance, and throughout his long life he lavished the utmost care on the selection and coaching of his interpreters and was never again prepared to make compromises in that respect. This time the effect came nowhere near his expectations, and the opera had only a short run. The Berlin performance, which took place a year later under his own direction, was a vast improvement, but in this instance the favourable reception on the part of the audience was neutralized by spiteful newspaper reports—another experience which remained decisive for Wagner's life: he was for ever after at war with his critics.

The sudden rise of the "vagabond" to general recognition also had its negative sides about which Wagner reports with a sense of humour:

The next consequence of this general estimation of my good fortune was a series of urgent requests to pay, and threatening dunning letters from those of my Königsberg creditors whom I had evaded in Riga by that disproportionately difficult and sorrowful flight. In addition everybody turned up who thought himself justified to make some demands on me, from anywhere and from long by-gone days, from the times I was still a student and even from my high-school years. Sometimes I exclaimed in amazement that I was expecting only one further bill: from my wet-nurse for suckling me.

It is almost disarming when one considers the air of injured innocence with which Wagner views each and every demand for repayment of a loan, and he considered himself justified in warding off such demands for as long as possible. First of all—and this has already been touched upon—*la* Schröder-Devrient had to help him with a matter of 1000 *Taler*. But then he had the brilliant idea of a lucrative enterprise for which he only needed one thing—money: he decided to have his operas printed himself in order not to have to share the profits with a publisher. The good-natured Schröder-Devrient agreed to join him in the venture but, warned by a friend, retracted her promise. Meanwhile plans had gone ahead, and both *Rienzi* and *Der fliegende Holländer* were published in full and vocal score by the Dresden music dealer Meser, who also undertook the distribution for a modest commission:

> With this development I entered into a vicious circle of entanglements and difficulties which, from then onwards, continued to dominate my life and which landed me in troubles which impressed their sad stamp on all my undertakings. It was quite clear that I was irrevocably involved in this enterprise, and the only hope for a satisfactory solution of the existing entanglements lay in continuing the venture and leading it to an assured success. So it became my continuous endeavour to raise money, first from friends, but soon, through sheer urgency, in any manner, even on short term and at excessive rates of interest—for this money was essential to continue the edition of my operas to which, obviously, *Tannhäuser* soon also had to be added. This just as an indication to prepare for those catastrophes towards which I was relentlessly drifting.

Wagner was disappointed that his operas did not make their way more quickly. But Dresden just was not Paris, and his

success was limited locally. *Rienzi* was staged in Hamburg and
Berlin, the *Holländer* in Riga and Kassel. But for the time being
that was it. In those days performing royalties did not yet exist,
and so his income from his operas was very sparse: a composer
sold his score for a moderate lump sum, and after that the opera
house in question had fulfilled all its financial obligations
towards him. The continued success of *Rienzi* in Dresden gained
Wagner much popularity, but he reaped no material harvest.

In his work as a conductor he found much greater satisfaction.
At his disposal was a vocal and orchestral apparatus of an
infinitely higher standard than that of those provincial theatres
in which he had begun, and he gave performances of a standard
which were not only highly appreciated by the public at large,
but even earned the personal praise of the music-loving
monarch. In Dresden Wagner became the great conductor who
was to be the shining example for a whole generation of young
artists: Hans von Bülow, Hans Richter, Felix Mottl, Anton
Seidl; and Wagner can truly be considered the ancestor of the
modern-style conductor. His work at the *Hoftheater* showed a
marked predilection for the operas of Gluck, Mozart, Beethoven
and Weber, and under his direction the concerts of the *Hofkapelle*, which until then had only been sporadic events, now
became a permanent institution. It was the Beethoven symphonies which formed the focal point of his interest. He had
always been fascinated by the Ninth. Because of under-rehearsed
performances it had been considered problematic and virtually
incomprehensible, but after painstaking preparation (in which
his Paris experiences stood him in good stead) he achieved a
sensational success with it. The amount of work he did during
those years is incredible. "By utmost industry and by starting
work in the early hours of the morning, even in winter" he
completed the *Tannhäuser* score in April 1845. In order to save
copyists' fees he himself wrote it out on paper prepared for
lithography—wrote it out in that wonderful characteristic hand
of his, the most beautiful composer's handwriting which has
ever existed—and had the score printed. He bubbled over with
ideas and all sorts of impulses. At his initiative the mortal
remains of Weber were exhumed in London and brought to
Dresden, the town of his one-time artistic sphere. For the

occasion he composed a Funeral Music, based on Weber motives, for eighty wind instruments and twenty muted drums. And he, the later revolutionary, planned a great procession of homage to greet the King after a prolonged absence: he got together 120 musicians and 300 singers, went with them to Pillnitz, and under the splendid sound of music which had been improvised in a matter of hours the King was treated to a march past in front of the royal palace. This piece became popular, and ten years later formed part of the repertoire of every military band; Wagner incorporated it in his *Tannhäuser* (on which he was working at the time) as the Entry of the Guests on the Wartburg.

Tannhäuser had its *première* on 19 October 1845. It was the most significant event of the Dresden years, that most fruitful period of Wagner's life. When his time was not absorbed by music, he dedicated himself to comprehensive literary studies. He had always been interested in the mediaeval cycles of legends, and this interest now led him to a closer study of the *Nibelungenlied*, and of the epics of Wolfram von Eschenbach and Gottfried von Strassburg, and these in turn directed his attention to the Germanic and Nordic myths which he came to know in the texts of Karl Simrock. With Wagner every impression turned into a picture, every picture into a dramatic scene. These years were the incubation period of his entire later output: *Der Ring des Nibelungen*, *Tristan und Isolde*, *Parsifal*, *Die Meistersinger von Nürnberg*, they all first took root in his fantasy at that time—quite apart from his work on *Lohengrin* which he tackled immediately after the *Tannhäuser* performance. The initial success of *Tannhäuser* was not as spontaneous and overwhelming as that of *Rienzi*, but it increased from performance to performance as experience improved the production and the public began to understand it. Eventually, like *Rienzi*, it became one of the most reliable props in the repertoire. It was also with *Tannhäuser* that Wagner recruited the first "Wagnerians", the first unquestioning adherents and enthusiasts who forever supported him—amongst them Hans von Bülow, then aged sixteen, on whose life he was to exert a decisive influence, and Frau Julie Ritter who, during the time of his Zürich exile, helped him with a not insignificant annual subsidy.

There is an incomparable witness for the elemental effect which *Tannhäuser* with its highly romantic world of fantasy had on contemporaries: Robert Schumann, who was then living in Dresden and who knew Wagner personally, although the two never really came close to each other. On 22 October 1845, after studying the *Tannhäuser* score, he wrote to Mendelssohn:

> . . . Now Wagner has gone and finished yet another opera—a brilliant chap, no doubt, full of fantastic ideas and daring to the extreme—the aristocracy is still enthusing about his *Rienzi*—but really, he cannot write or think as much as four bars that are good, let alone beautiful . . . and now the whole score is issued, beautifully printed—with fifths and octaves galore—and now he would like to alter and erase—too late! . . .

But a few weeks later Schumann heard a performance and again wrote to Mendelssohn: "Perhaps soon we can talk about *Tannhäuser*. I must retract much of what I wrote to you after having merely read the score. Seen on the stage it is all quite different, and I was often deeply moved"—and to Heinrich Dorn on 7 January 1846:

> I wish you could see Wagner's *Tannhäuser*. It has depth, originality, and much of it is a hundred times better than his earlier operas—although there are also moments of musical triviality. By and large, he may become of great importance for the theatre, and from what I know of him, he has it in him. The technical side and the orchestration I find excellent, more masterly by far than before.

A splendid testimonial for *Tannhäuser*, and just as splendid a testimonial for the honesty and sensibility of the author of those letters, to whom this must have been a totally alien world.

While at work on *Tannhäuser* a little episode occurred about which Wagner reports with humour and subtle characterization: Dresden received the visit of Spontini who, as Meyerbeer's predecessor, had introduced the most resplendent period of Parisian *grand opéra*. Once famous, he now belonged to the

category of also-rans. Wagner invited Spontini to a performance
of *La Vestale*, his most famous opera, which was just being
rehearsed at the *Hoftheater*. The "Master" came, took over the
baton quite unceremoniously, and after all sorts of initial
difficulties gave a magnificent performance of the work which
even then was already slightly antiquated. Wagner tells of many
conversations which he had with the visiting celebrity, but the
one which is particularly remarkable is that in which Spontini
quite seriously warns his young German colleague that he
should not write operas:

> When I heard your *Rienzi* I said to myself: this is a brilliant
> man, but he has already done more than his due. . . . How
> can you demand of anybody to create something new when
> I, Spontini, declare to you that beyond my earlier works I
> am incapable of achieving a further improvement, and when
> there can be no doubt whatsoever that since *La Vestale* no
> single note has been written which has not been stolen out
> of one of my scores?

He kindly offered to stay in Dresden to perform the sum total
of his operatic output—and Wagner was the happiest man on
earth when the conferment of some papal honour and of a
Danish medal forced the irksome guest to take his reluctant
leave. Wagner concludes: "Both I and Röckel [his assistant and
chorus master] fervently praised the Holy Father and the King
of Denmark. Full of emotion we bade farewell to the peculiar
Master and, in order to make him completely happy, I promised
him that I would give serious thought to his friendly advice as
regards the composing of operas."

Like a burlesque interlude, this gay intermezzo interrupts the
dramatic events, the turning point of which, as in classic drama,
sets in immediately after the *Tannhäuser* climax and seems to be
driven forward with the fury of an inescapable destiny.

> Not only did I finally have to start repaying all those loans
> which, under ever increasing sacrifices, I had had to make
> for the precious edition of my operas, but as I had been
> forced in the end to enlist the assistance of usurers, the rumour

of my indebtedness had spread so far that even friends who had helped me when I was settling in Dresden were getting extremely worried in all matters concerning me. The most saddening experience I had with Frau Schröder-Devrient who, by her incredibly inconsiderate behaviour, precipitated the catastrophe.

As Wagner himself reports, it was his own niece Johanna Wagner, aged eighteen, who had charmed everyone as Elisabeth in *Tannhäuser*, who was the cause of the feelings of Schröder-Devrient towards him becoming noticeably frigid, as it was he who had brought the successful young rival to Dresden. She sued Wagner for her 1000 *Taler*, and he was forced to inform the *Intendant*, von Lüttichau, of his precarious financial position. Von Lüttichau was on Wagner's side and granted his request for an advance, which came out of the theatre's pension fund. But Wagner saw himself "enticed to omit from his application such of his debts which were not of a hostile nature and which he thought he would eventually be able to settle out of the expected incomes from his publishing enterprise". In this respect his attitude never altered. Many years later, when his debts had grown to the size of an avalanche, he handled matters in exactly the same manner with the King of Bavaria, who was willing to act as his guarantor; even on the eve of the Munich first performance of *Tristan* (1865) Wagner was threatened with distraint on account of an old debt and was compelled to run to the King for assistance. To Wagner, a creditor who stood on his rights was an immoral, despicable character; a creditor who did not could safely be ignored.

It must be admitted that a benefactor was no better off than a creditor. Because of his over-sensitive *amour-propre* and the humiliations suffered during his youth he could not but react with hostility towards all obligations, no matter to whom they were due. This is also at the root of his attitude to Meyerbeer. Like Schumann before him (in a well-known article on *Les Huguenots*) Wagner had every reason to reject Meyerbeer unconditionally on artistic grounds, but his rude attacks on him were dishonourable and malicious and went far beyond what is permissible in unbiased criticism.

As once upon a time in Riga, Wagner's last years in Dresden were characterized by a state of progressively increasing irritability. Once again the primary cause was his indebtedness, but another reason for his rebellious mood against the existing conditions was an increasing realization of his artistic dissatisfaction. To this must be added an external factor which, like a catalyst in a chemical reaction, led to the explosion of the accumulated destructive elements: the latent revolutionary excitement which, after the Paris uprising of 1848, permeated Vienna, Munich and the whole of Germany and was reaching a flash-point. It is a marvel of his creative nature that even then he could still withdraw into an ivory tower where he was unassailable: whenever musically inspired, he simply shrugged off all mundane problems. He might neglect the duties of his position, he might forget all his debts, but his creative work was sacred to him. Every hour of leisure was dedicated to his work on *Lohengrin*, which he kept up irrespective, and by the time of the March revolution in Vienna the score was completed. The performance of the new work was scheduled for the following season, designs for costumes and stage sets were well in hand. But now his devil took over. The many public discussions about democracy, monarchy and republican ideals provoked him to write an article, *Republik und Monarchie*, which was first published anonymously. It culminated in the rhetorical question whether it might not be possible to carry out all necessary reforms with a king as head of state. This essay, in which he assigned to the king the position of crowned president of a republic, he read to a public meeting of 3000 people "with emphatic determination. The result of this was quite terrifying. It seemed that nothing stuck in the minds of the audience of the Royal *Kapellmeister* more than his occasional derogatory remarks about the sycophants at the Royal Court." As if this was not enough he now handed to the *Intendant*, von Lüttichau, one of the sycophants, a draft for a reorganization of the *Hoftheater* along the lines of his idealistic and artistic aims. In this draft he very kindly sacks the *Intendant*, "promotes" his senior colleague Reissiger to the completely innocuous domain of church music—and with equal generosity he offers to take over himself the responsibilities of the entire management. Incidentally, when many years later he incorporated this draft in his Collected Writings, he excised these little details from the original text. The reaction to all this is not particularly surprising: *Lohengrin* went by the board, and all preparations came to an immediate standstill. This removed the last of Wagner's inhibitions. He made a confidant of Röckel who was just as badly indebted and in addition lumbered with a family of six whom he had to support. Röckel caused a revolutionary tract to be printed, was accused of high treason and promptly dismissed from the *Hoftheater*. Röckel was a follower of the socialist trends which had spread from Paris. While legal proceedings against him were still only in a preparatory stage, he became editor of a radical democratic weekly to which Wagner contributed several anonymous articles, though his authorship was perfectly obvious to everyone.

I now took my walks in complete solitude and gained great peace of mind, working out in my head visions of a condition of human society, and at that time it was only the socialists and communists, then so active in building up their system with highest hopes and every ounce of energy, who furnished a general basis for those visions. But these endeavours only acquired sense and meaning for me when they had reached their ends, the goal of their political upheavals and constructions. From then onwards I, on my part, could begin with my own reconstruction in the cause of art.

It is amazing with what forbearance the management of the *Hoftheater* treated its *Kapellmeister* who was so active in such directions, and the fact that he was not suspended must be ascribed to the extraordinary prestige which the composer of *Rienzi* and *Tannhäuser* enjoyed in Dresden. He had only to suffer one single expression of disapproval: the concerts of the *Hofkapelle* which he had instituted were entrusted to the direction of Reissiger.

But now a new protagonist came on to the Wagnerian stage in the person of the Russian anarchist Michael Bakunin who, in those years, appeared as a stormy petrel of revolution wherever there was a chance of creating unrest. Wagner gives a masterly description of this strange man: "When I first met him in the shabby care of the Röckels I was truly surprised by the odd but imposing personality of that man who was then at the prime of his thirties. Everything about him was over-dimensional, emanating a latent energy of primitive vitality." For Wagner's idealistically-artistic endeavour Bakunin had one single solution of charming simplicity: murder and destruction. A new and better world could only be built up on the ruins of the old. For once Wagner met someone who, as far as loquacity was concerned, could beat him at his own game. With his customary vivacity he tried to tell the guest all about some new opera project, but did not succeed in arousing much interest. "Regarding the music he advised me, in all manner of variation, to set but one text: the tenor should sing 'Off with his head', the soprano 'String him up' and the bass 'Fire, fire'." Wagner, intrepid as he was, compelled him to listen to some of *Der fliegende Holländer*, and Bakunin was decidedly impressed, which pleased Wagner no end. And he tells:

> He had to lead the miserable life of a fugitive who has to go from hiding place to hiding place, and so occasionally I invited him to have supper at my home. My wife set platters of dainty cut meat and sausage on the table which he promptly gulped down by the pound, not frugally spreading them on bread as is customary in Saxony. [Minna must have been aghast!] This and other unimportant habits proved that within this curious person a completely anti-cultural wildness lived side by side with demands for the purest ideals of humanity, and in my contact with him my impressions ever oscillated between instinctive terror and irresistible attraction. . . . As he incessantly demanded destruction and again destruction, I finally had to ask myself how my weird friend was planning to set all this destruction into motion. As it turned out, as I then already sensed, and as soon it became perfectly apparent, all the unconditional action which this man stipulated was based on the most irrational of hypotheses. . . . My hopes for the artistic future of human society may have appeared completely impractical and as insubstantial as air, but it was soon crystal clear that his own concepts regarding the

imperative destruction of all existing cultural institutions were at least no less unfounded.

As so often happens in this type of crisis, the forces fighting for reform were far too disunited and disorganized to achieve more than chance successes. The only point on which democrats, socialists and anarchists could agree was opposition to the prevailing establishment and authority. In Austria as in Prussia the revolutionary movement was virtually wiped out by the end of the year, although this does not mean that the ferment had ceased. Wagner was gloomy and disappointed and felt himself more and more in isolation.

From now on I lived in a state of twilight, of restive brooding, expectant, yet without desire. It was clear to me that my artistic activity in Dresden was drawing to a close, and also that my position there was a burden of which I wanted to rid myself—it only needed an external cause for me to do so. On the other hand the entire political situation in Germany as in Saxony was drawing near to inevitable catastrophe: it came closer with every day, and it pleased me to imagine that my personal fate was intertwined with this general development.

March brings the one and only ray of sunshine: a letter from Liszt, who has taken over the musical direction of the *Hoftheater* in Weimar. He admires Wagner with whom, at occasional meetings in Berlin and Dresden, he has also come into personal contact. Now, as the first after Dresden, he prepares a *Tannhäuser* production. A few weeks later he can inform the composer of the success of the work and invites him to a performance—the third—at the beginning of May.

But just before then the long-awaited storm was unleashed by the dissolution of the Chamber of Deputies—the beginning of a fierce reaction. Röckel who, as a member of the Chamber, had enjoyed immunity now had to flee, and Wagner stepped in, taking over not only the responsibility for the family Röckel left behind, but also the editorship of his pamphlet. On 3 May matters came to a head with an armed insurrection.

Wagner's description of those revolutionary days in Dresden deserves a place amongst the masterpieces of German prose style. But his own behaviour in this time of stress, about which he speaks with clear objectivity and after many years had passed, borders on feeble-mindedness. Of course the general excitement must have been incredible; but Wagner simply had to be in on everything: we find him on the barricades when army and militia are clashing; at the town hall where the revolutionary movement has its headquarters; and when the old opera house (where only a few weeks ago he had conducted Beethoven's Ninth) stood in flames one of the revolutionary militia-men shouted at him: "*Herr Kapellmeister*, the 'beautiful spark of the Gods' has sparked it off all right!"—in allusion to Schiller's text *Freude, schöner Götterfunke* in the Finale of the Ninth. Röckel came back and requisitioned rifles wherever he could get hold of them. Bakunin was in his element and perfectly happy. A provisional government was formed with the Freiberg district administrator Heubner at its head. There was little fear of the Saxon army, but much more of the Prussian troops who were approaching in order to restore law and order. Wagner went to the printer of Röckel's *Volksblatt* and had a slogan, addressed to the Saxon soldiery, printed on strips of paper: "Are you with us against foreign troops?", and the barricades were plastered with them. But this seems to be the only act of high treason he committed—at least it is the only one to which he admits. For the rest, what he tells about himself gives the impression that he was an indefatigable camp-follower:

> I felt no urge and certainly no vocation to apportion to myself any sort of role or function; nevertheless I quite consciously let go of every consideration of my personal affairs and decided to allow myself to drift with a desperate feeling of ease on the tide of those events into which my own attitude had driven me.

As part of the town had already been occupied by Prussian troops he took his wife to Chemnitz to his married sister Klara. To the horror of his relatives he himself returned to Dresden, found the town in a state of chaos and destruction, and had to make his way over the rubble, from barricade to barricade. At this juncture Wagner's account gives an incomparably vivid description of the fantastic confusion and disorder brought about by such circumstances. Bakunin, implacably determined to offer resistance to the last, gave Wagner a report on the state of affairs: "He said that early that morning he had had the newly planted trees in the Maximilians-Allee felled to provide entanglements and thus protect himself against cavalry attack on his flank. What particularly amused him was the woe of the residents of this avenue who had loudly bemoaned only the loss of the lovely trees." But the fighters on the barricades were utterly exhausted, their leaders kept issuing contradictory orders, and resistance against the better-equipped regular army seemed hopeless. Heubner and Bakunin requisitioned a carriage with which they wanted to beat their retreat to the Erzgebirge, and Wagner joined them with the intention of returning to Chemnitz. But—and this turned out to be most fortunate for him—he lost his travelling companions when making a break in their journey and reached his destination in some other conveyance. Heubner and Bakunin had arrived before him and had been unceremoniously arrested by the constabulary, a fate which Wagner would have shared if he had been caught in their company. His brother-in-law now took him through the night to Altenburg, from where he proceeded by stage coach to Weimar. He writes:

At that time I was in a dream-like state of detachment, and I cannot better describe it than by saying that at this first renewed meeting with Liszt I gave the appearance that I immediately wanted to enter into discussion on the only subject which concerned him in connection with me, namely the impending next performance of *Tannhäuser*. It was not easy to acquaint my friend with the fact that, as Court *Kapellmeister*, I had not left Dresden in a quite regular manner. In truth, my notions about my relationship to the judicial authorities of my home country were not very clear. Had I committed a breach of the law or not? I found it impossible to come to any sort of definite conclusion.

The question was soon answered without any ambiguity whatsoever. The answer consisted of a warrant for Wagner's arrest on the charge of high treason, a warrant which threatened him with immediate arrest in all the territories of the German Confederation. It can be assumed that Liszt first of all told his friend off in no uncertain terms, but then assisted him with circumspection and characteristic generosity. Wagner was kept in hiding in order to await a visit of his despairing Minna, whom he wanted to see at all costs. She came and talked him into fleeing immediately. "No attempt on my part to attune her to my views was of any avail. She insisted that she could only look on me as an ill-advised and rash individual who had landed himself as well as her in a horrible dilemma." Liszt's emphatic advice was for him to go to Paris where he would have the best chances of success, as now he would arrive with an entirely different background than on the occasion of that first ill-starred sojourn in the French capital. He raised 2000 francs to give Wagner a start, and with a forged passport Wagner got safely to Switzerland by way of Bavaria, stayed in Zürich for a short while and continued his journey to Paris in early June. In the *Journal des Débats* Liszt had published an article about Wagner which had aroused much attention, and he had also given him a recommendation to his agent Belloni in Paris, so that he had really done his best to pave the way for him.

4

EXILE

(1849–1861)

WAGNER HAD BURNT his boats, but it was only gradually that he became fully aware of the consequences of his actions. He had followed Liszt's advice to go to Paris because he had no idea what else to do. But perhaps Liszt did not yet know his friend well enough. Having grown up in Paris and being half a Frenchman, a diplomat and cosmopolitan of captivating manners, Liszt was at perfect ease in the elegant glitter of the Paris *salons*. Wagner was just plain Wagner, and he felt out of place in that world, despite Belloni's help and practical suggestions. As his hatred of Meyerbeer had already reached full fruition, he saw his finger at each and every turn and ascribed every set-back to his machinations. His personal feelings were violently opposed to Liszt's idea of writing a French opera for Paris. The fact that a cholera epidemic was spreading through Paris did not make his stay any more pleasant, and so he returned to Zürich where he arrived with his last twenty francs and claimed the temporary hospitality of an acquaintance, the musician Alexander Müller. He also asked Minna, who had returned to Dresden, to join him there and was bitterly disappointed at her hesitation. He could not and would not understand that Minna considered him responsible for all her misfortunes, for her degradation from the respected position of *Frau Hofkapellmeister* to that of the poor mendicant of those terrible earlier days, and that in his course of action she could not see anything but criminal and irresponsible rashness. Although finally Minna allowed herself to be persuaded and joined her husband in Zürich, it may be assumed that from then onwards their marriage was irretrievably ruined. Once again Liszt had to foot the bill for the journey. But Wagner obviously had outgrown her in every respect. Erotically he was only too ready for new adventures, especially as in comparison with his tremendous vitality Minna with her forty years was aged and worn out before her time; and with her intellectual limitations she could not cope with the problems confronting her as the wife of a genius. Nevertheless she arrived with her *soi-disant* sister Natalie, one dog and one parrot, all of whom had formed part and parcel of the Dresden *ménage*, and with her extraordinary housewifely mentality she managed to create a modest but cosy home. Soon the exiles found contacts and stimulating acquaintances in a circle of new friends: the civil servant Jakob Sulzer, the then completely unknown author Gottfried Keller, the editor Bernhard Spyri, the musicians Alexander Müller and Wilhelm Baumgartner, the architect Gottfried Semper, the poet Georg Herwegh. The only burning and unsolved question was: what were they going to live on?

Wagner answered questions of this sort in a simple and radical manner from which he never deviated. Music to him would never again become a means of earning a living; that would be an ethical offence against his innermost vocation. It was his predestined task in life to create immortal masterpieces, and it was up to the world to provide the wherewithal for him to live—and live very well and comfortably at that. For this design he had to find a pattern, be it through artistically-minded sovereigns, through self-sacrificing sponsors, or through an organization of some kind. He knocked on Liszt's door in order to make a deal with the *Grossherzog* of Weimar: if the Grand Duke were to grant him an annuity, he (Wagner) would guarantee that the Weimar *Hoftheater* should have the rights to all first performances of his future *œuvre*. This did not come off, since, after all that had happened, none of the German princes were very favourably disposed towards Wagner. Next he approached his friend Heine in Dresden with the proposition that he should recruit the admirers of Wagner's art for the idea of instituting a large-scale operation to create a "charitable fund" for his purpose, and he was most amazed to hear that there was but little sympathy for "that hot-head of the barricades". However, a Dresden friend, Frau Julie Ritter, offered the exile an annuity of 500 *Taler*, and a wealthy Englishwoman, Mrs Taylor, who had made the acquaintance of Wagner in the circle of the Ritter family in Dresden, was prepared to guarantee him 3000 francs annually. The Weimar theatre offered him an advance of 500 *Taler* for a new opera, *Siegfried*, for which he had completed the text and had promised that the score would be ready within a period of twelve months. So for the time being the wolf had been averted from the door.

The events of that last year had thrown Wagner into an inner conflict which possibly was more profound than he himself realized at the time. Free at last from the burden of material obligations, he was determined to dedicate all his energies to his compositions. But suddenly strange inhibitions made themselves felt and, instead of composing, he took refuge in theoretical writing. In the summer of 1849 he wrote an essay *Die Kunst und die Revolution* ("Art and Revolution") in which he tried to find a generally valid formula for his own clash with his surroundings. The following two years were, in the main, dedicated to two major works, *Das Kunstwerk der Zukunft* ("The Work of Art of the Future") and *Oper und Drama*, in which at great length he amplified his artistic theories and ideas. Both these works were of fundamental importance as an attempt to clarify within his own mind, in an historical as well as an aesthetic respect, all those ideas which up to then he had pursued instinctively, and at the same time to find an utterly new definition of the ultimate aims of his artistic output. More will have to be said about these works, as also about *Das Judentum in der Musik* ("Judaism in Music"), a pamphlet which he published under the pseudonym K. Freigedank ["K. Freethinker"]. This pamphlet caused quite a sensation, and the true name of its author did not remain a secret for very long.

In addition Wagner was full of plans for new operas. One of these, the *Siegfried* mentioned earlier on, developed into enormous proportions, the result of combining the Siegfried legend with elements of Germanic mythology. *Siegfrieds Tod* ("Siegfried's Death"), as he first sketched it, necessitated another drama to precede it, *Der junge Siegfried* ("The Young Siegfried"). In the last act of this, however, the sleeping Brünnhilde made her appearance, and had first to be introduced as *Die Walküre* ("The Valkyrie"), and Wotan's highly complex position in this Brünnhilde drama demanded some sort of explanation of how all this had come about: *Das Rheingold*. Thus the overall concept of this monumental work came into being in a retrograde manner. Apart from all his other studies Wagner had devoted himself intensively to Greek drama during his Dresden years, above all to Aeschylus and Sophocles, and the form of the trilogy—which now he enlarged to that of a tetralogy—came naturally to him as a fundamental of a large-scale dramatic construction. In his theoretical writings his train of thought was guided by these basic principles of Greek drama, but it must be assumed that his ideas were influenced by the maturing plan of his tetralogy rather than that this latter had resulted from his theories.

Of course, at that time this concept, from which later *Der Ring des Nibelungen* was to develop, was finalized only in its essentials. Wagner's unfailing instinct apparently resisted the temptation to make a rash and hasty start on a composition for which he did not yet feel himself ready and sufficiently disengaged. His inner unrest was reflected in his contradictory decisions. February 1850 saw him in Paris again where, despite all his objections, he intended to investigate the possibility of writing a French opera and, as it was planned to perform his *Tannhäuser* Overture, a suitable point of contact offered itself to him. But the only result of this journey was another of those fantastic adventures which almost led to a renewed crisis, to yet one more flight. In his memoirs Wagner is reticent and only touches on those events most discreetly, but there is sufficient evidence in his correspondence of those days with Minna to make matters clear. When in Dresden Wagner had made the acquaintance of Mrs Taylor, who now offered him an annuity; she was accompanied by her young daughter Jessie. Both had been lastingly impressed by Wagner, and particularly by *Tannhäuser*. When Jessie, who meanwhile had married the wine merchant Laussot, came to know that he was in Paris, she invited Wagner to Bordeaux where they were living. He accepted the invitation and stayed with the Laussots for three weeks, constantly making music with Jessie, who was an excellent pianist and also showed much understanding for Wagner's literary plans. It would appear that feelings of great

passion developed between the two, and Wagner, on his return
to Paris, wrote to Minna of his irrevocable decision to leave her
and "to escape from this world". Minna, terrified—for obviously
she knew what such a flight implied—immediately made her
way to Paris, where Wagner had instructed his friend Kietz to
say that he was not available, and Wagner went to Geneva to
await further developments. Minna had guessed correctly: he
had proposed to Jessie to flee to Greece or Asia Minor with him
in order to start a new life together, far removed from the
decadence of western culture, and Jessie seemed prepared to
follow him. But in the meantime Mrs Taylor had scented the
affair and did her best to straighten out her daughter. Monsieur
Laussot, informed about the whole intrigue, swore to shoot the
blackguard. Wagner, who had had a short note from Jessie
telling him of her change of mind, promptly returned to Bordeaux
with the firm conviction that, with his eloquence, he would be
able to convince the jealous husband that he had no moral
right to a wife who was in love with another man. But the
Laussots had left Bordeaux, and on his arrival the police told
Wagner in no uncertain terms that he had no business there and
should leave the place post-haste. With this the affair had
reached its ignominious end. Wagner, who had been counting
on an imminent payment from Mrs Taylor for his "escape from
this world", went back home after some hesitation and made
his peace with Minna. Naturally the Taylor annuity was now
forfeit, but once again his guardian angel had preserved him
from the worst, just as he had saved him from the penal
servitude to which Heubner and Röckel had been condemned.
Bakunin was extradited to Russia and then sent to Siberia.

    In the same year another event brought about an important
turn in Wagner's fortunes: in August Liszt conducted the first
performance of *Lohengrin* in Weimar, and the effect of this act
of friendship proved to be lasting. It was courageous, as
musical director of a *Hoftheater*, to stage the work of one who
was under warrant of arrest, but the effect justified Liszt's
daring. The fact that a theatre with the relatively modest
means of that in Weimar could successfully stage a Wagner
opera encouraged other adventurous opera directors to try their
luck with one or other of those works about which latterly so

much had been said and written—for in those respects both Wagner and Liszt had been indefatigable. First it was *Tannhäuser*, then *Lohengrin* which took one operatic stage after the other by storm, and both works took a permanent place in the repertoire, a rare event at a time of meagre production in the field of German opera.

Der fliegende Holländer soon followed the other two, and finally even *Rienzi*, although the unaccustomed difficulties of its stage requirements impeded its progress. As has already been explained, the income from these performances was nowhere near as much as one might assume—on average Wagner received twenty to thirty *Napoléons d'or* for each of his scores as sole payment—but still, there was always some source of income. That money had a habit of melting in his hand like snow under the noonday sun was a different matter: he never knew how to hang on to it. A mere century later, at a similar stage of his career, he would have been able to live in princely fashion on the royalties accruing from his works. Ten years after the first *Lohengrin* performance he could boast that he was the only German who had not seen the work yet: he still could not show his face in Germany.

Now the Zürich friends also wanted to hear something from Wagner, and he allowed himself to be persuaded to give some orchestral concerts, mainly dedicated to Beethoven symphonies, with inadequate local forces. At the Zürich theatre he had thoughtlessly given a guarantee when they had engaged Karl Ritter (son of Julie Ritter) as musical director on his recommendation. When his protégé proved a complete failure, Wagner was forced to deputize as conductor, but a visit of the young Hans von Bülow, a friend of Ritter's, saved him from this embarrassment: Bülow took over the baton, immediately proved himself a born conductor, was happy to step into the shoes of Karl Ritter—and thereby began that career which had been the wish of his heart and from which only the opposition of his parents had deterred him. The Zürich theatre with its exceedingly modest means did not afford Wagner much satisfaction, but finally, grudgingly, he allowed his *Holländer* to be performed. In May 1853 he even put on his own little music festival: three evenings, during which he performed excerpts from *Der fliegende Holländer, Tannhäuser* and *Lohengrin*, in the main with musicians whom he had invited from Germany. It was a costly venture which brought him enormous success, and Wagner now became the centre of interest in the whole of Switzerland. For quite some time this was his last venture of a practical nature, for now, after five years of artistic pause, his creativity flooded forth again in full spate, and all his other interests receded into the background. The text of *Der Ring des Nibelungen*, (*Das Rheingold, Die Walküre, Siegfried, Götterdämmerung*) he had completed in November 1852, but he was still in doubt, he still felt insecure faced with the task of tackling the composition of such an enormous work, still lacking self-confidence vis-à-vis his own powers of invention after such a long complete break from all compositional activity. So he hoped for the necessary stimulus from a journey to Italy which he had been envisaging for a long time. Via Turin he went to Genoa and from there to La Spezia, where he fell prey to some febrile illness.

I succumbed to a trance-like condition in which I suddenly had the emotion as though I were sinking into rapidly flowing water. Soon the rushing sound of this water was transmuted in my ears into the musical sound of an E flat major chord which persistently surged up and down in a broken figuration. This broken chord developed in melodic figurations of increasing intensity, but the pure triad of E flat never altered, and by its very insistence it seemed to lend to the element in which I was being submerged an infinity of meaning. With a sudden start I awoke from my semi-slumber and had a feeling as though the waves were rushing high above me. I realized immediately that the orchestral prelude to *Rheingold* as I had been bearing it within me without yet being able to give it a clear definition had come to full fruition. Equally quickly I also comprehended how matters were to be with me: the life impulse would never flow towards me from without, but always from within my own self.

He curtailed his journey and returned to Zürich by the shortest route. A meeting in Basle with Liszt, whom he even accompanied to Paris, caused another unavoidable delay, but by the beginning of 1853 he could really begin composing. In the short space of ten weeks, working feverishly, he completed the sketch of the *Rheingold* music; only five months later the score was finished. By July 1854 he had begun the composition of *Walküre* and completed it as a sketch before the end of the year.

Then came an interruption. Tempted by a sizeable fee, Wagner accepted the offer to conduct a season of the Philharmonic Society in London consisting of a series of eight concerts at two-weekly intervals. What is interesting about this offer is that it shows clearly what a European celebrity Wagner had become. Arriving in London in early March, he soon regretted having come at all. The orchestra was good, but rehearsal was insufficient, the programmes rarely to his taste, the London critics malicious, and the climate, to him, unbearable. The public took to him very warm-heartedly and his own music—excerpts from *Lohengrin* and the *Tannhäuser* Overture— was received with great applause. At the royal request of Queen Victoria the *Tannhäuser* Overture had to be played again when she attended one of the Wagner concerts with her husband Prince Albert. Of the things Wagner has to report about this London visit only one point is of major interest: he came into closer contact with Hector Berlioz who was conducting a competitive enterprise, the New Philharmonic Society, and now they became acquainted personally, although the two men hardly ever really understood each other. What Wagner has to tell about one of their discussions is unintentionally humorous, because he never noticed the irony, the *esprit* with which his French colleague countered Wagner's verbosity regarding the esoterics of artistic conception.

I attempted to define the impulses of the life forces on our souls, which then keep us prisoner in their way, until we can completely free ourselves from them in the only possible manner: by developing the innermost strength of our spiritual self. But this strength must not be called forth by such impressions: it must be awoken from the deepest slumber, so that the images of our art will never appear as

the effect of this life impulse, but on the contrary as a
liberation from that self-same impulse. At this point Berlioz
smiled as though with understanding condescension and
said: *Nous appelons celà: digérer.* (We call that digestion.)

Wagner's bombast must have afforded him considerable
amusement!

Another London meeting was with Karl Klindworth, a pupil
of Liszt and an excellent pianist, who offered to make a piano
arrangement of the vocal score of *Rheingold*. Embarrassment
must also have been a dominating factor when Wagner met
Meyerbeer again, considering the malicious manner in which
Wagner had attacked his erstwhile benefactor in his writings.
"Meyerbeer was completely paralysed when he saw me, which
on the other hand put me into such a state of mind that we
could not exchange one single word. . . . Howard [the mutual
acquaintance at whose home this meeting occurred] shook his
head and could not understand that 'two great composers
could meet in such a peculiar manner'."

Having suffered through his eight concerts, Wagner was
happy to turn his back on the Rainy Isles. Slowly work on the
score of *Die Walküre*, which had been interrupted by his
English enterprise, got under way again and by March 1856
the great work was completed in its final copy. Six months
later he started *Siegfried*, where he met some obstacles. He
completed the first act in February 1857, then sketched the
second act without bringing it to the stage of a full score. After
that he decided to put the composition aside for the time being.

This decision was apparently dictated in equal measure by
internal as well as external causes. Ever since Wagner had
seriously started work on his tetralogy he had been fully
aware of the problems of bringing a work of such dimensions
to a performance, especially taking into consideration the
enormous demands made on the sheer technicalities of staging
it. His little Zürich music festival may have been a minor
attempt to gauge matters—to see whether one could risk a
major operation there and assemble the necessary artistic
forces. From a letter to his Dresden friend Theodor Uhlig we
can glean the general trend of his thoughts:

In order to realize the best, the most decisive and most important which I can achieve under the existing conditions and thereby to reach what to me quite clearly is the dominant task of my life, I need a matter of perhaps 10,000 *Taler*. Should I ever be able to dispose of such a sum, I would do the following: here, where I now happen to live and where many things are not all that bad, I would have a rough theatre built of boards and beams, according to my own plans, on a lovely meadow outside the town and would only have it furnished with the *décor* and stage machinery needed for a *Siegfried* performance. I would then choose the most suitable singers to be found and invite them to Zürich for six weeks; the major part of the chorus I would try to gather from local amateurs, for there are fine voices and strong, healthy people to be found here. Similarly I would assemble an orchestra. At the beginning of the new year, in all the newspapers of Germany, I would then issue subscriptions and invitations to friends of musical drama to attend my intended Music Drama Festival. ... Once everything was organized, I would allow three performances to take place; after the third the theatre would be demolished and my score burnt. ... You will probably think me completely mad. Maybe, but I assure you that it is the only hope of my life to achieve this, and this prospect alone can entice me to embark on the composition of a great work. So, please get me 10,000 *Taler*—that's all!

One may smile indulgently at this grandiose gesture (surely Wagner was not quite serious about burning the score?), but one must admire the incredible singleness of purpose with which this fanatic stuck to a plan which here he had only outlined in an improvisatory way and which, twenty-five years later, he turned into a concrete reality in connection with the work which then had only been jotted down as a rough sketch—for his Bayreuth theatre was specifically built to perform the *Ring*. But the 10,000 *Taler* simply could not be found, and in any case the venture would probably have cost infinitely more. When he was working on the music of *Siegfried* Wagner had abandoned his ideas anyway, at least as far as Zürich was concerned. During those years he had often come together with Liszt, who had studied the scores of *Rheingold* and *Die Walküre* with great enthusiasm, and probably he had not made a secret of his own doubts concerning the practicality of performing the tetralogy as an entity.

The first spate of creative inspiration had been poured into *Rheingold* and *Die Walküre*, and after the ecstasy of the second of these works, especially with its deeply moving human tragedy, it is conceivable that for the time being at least Wagner could not raise himself to the same level of intensity for his *Siegfried*. He must have noticed a certain relaxation of his inner tension, much though his fantasy was enthralled with the character of the young Siegfried whose main scenes (in Mime's forge and in the forest) became the most inspired moments of the first and second acts. What turned the scales was that Breitkopf & Härtel of Leipzig, who had published *Lohengrin*, could not make up their minds to take on the *Ring*, and in a letter of 28 June 1857 Wagner wrote to Liszt:

With Härtels I shall have no more trouble as I have finally decided to abandon my stubborn intention of completing my *Ring*. I have still been able to lead my young Siegfried into the beautiful solitude of the forest; there, under a linden-tree, I have left him and bid him farewell with tears in my eyes: he is better off there than elsewhere. . . . I really only needed this dispute with the Härtels—my first contact with that world which might have made the realization of my undertaking possible—to bring me finally to my senses and make me aware that my whole concept was nothing but a big chimera.

But something else had happened. A new subject had seized his imagination, a subject which had preoccupied him as early as his Dresden days and for which he now had become sufficiently mature: *Tristan und Isolde*. Fantast that he was, he was persuaded by some chatterbox who visited him that the Emperor of Brazil, Don Pedro, was interested in his music, and on the strength of this gossip he immediately formulated a new plan.

As he wrote to Liszt, he was considering, with *Tristan*, to create a work

> of lesser dimensions in order to facilitate performances. In addition I have another curious idea. I am thinking of having a good Italian translation provided for this work, so that I may offer it to the theatre of Rio de Janeiro—where probably they will already have performed my *Tannhäuser* by then—for first performance as an Italian opera. I shall dedicate the work to the Emperor of Brazil who soon will receive copies of my last three operas, and I think that all this will bring in enough that I may live unmolested for some little time.

This gossip who called himself Brazilian Consul accepted the expensively bound copies, complete with dedication, in order to pass them on to the Emperor. If the Emperor ever received them, he must have been mightily astounded. Be that as it may, Wagner heard no more of the Consul, the Emperor of Brazil, nor of his precious vocal scores.

As is well known Wagner was equally in error in his supposition that *Tristan* would be a simpler, more easily performable opera. Once again his demon had got hold of him—that demon which knew no quarter, neither on the stage nor in life. Once again Wagner had become enmeshed in a passionate love affair which reached its critical point in the spring of 1858. For quite a few years the Wesendoncks had belonged to the Wagner circle. Otto Wesendonck, a wealthy industrialist from the Rhineland, had settled in Zürich with his charming young wife Mathilde and their two children. He proved a generous patron to the notoriously impecunious Wagner, and when the flow of money from Frau Ritter dried up for a variety of reasons he proved himself an open-handed, ever-ready friend, and it was he who bore the main financial brunt of the little "Wagner Festival" in Zürich which has been mentioned earlier. The Wesendoncks settled in the immediate vicinity of Zürich where they built a magnificent villa, and they gave Wagner the use of a simple country house which stood in their grounds. Together with Minna, Wagner moved in at Easter 1857; he called it his "haven" and was quite prepared to remain in occupancy for the rest of his days. On 8 May he wrote to Liszt:

> Ten days ago we moved into the little country house near the W.'s villa, which I owe to the truly great understanding and friendship of that family. . . . For the time being everything is furnished and made comfortable according to my wishes and needs; everything is in place as it should be. My study has been arranged in the pedantic and elegant manner which is well known to you: my writing desk stands under the big window with a magnificent view of the lake and the alps, and peace and tranquillity surround me. There is a pretty and quite well-looked-after garden inviting me to little walks and restful contemplation, and to my wife it gives that pleasant occupation of airing her fads about me. There is also a fairly big vegetable garden which requires her most tender care. As you can see, I have found a pleasant place for my seclusion, and if I consider how long I have yearned for this, and how difficult it had been to visualize the mere prospect of it, I feel constrained to recognize this good W. as my greatest benefactor.

We well know what attitude Wagner took towards his benefactors. In his memoirs he voices decidedly unfriendly feelings towards "this good Wesendonck", and he says very little of his relationship to Mathilde. But his letters of that time give a clear idea that it must have been most passionate, especially those to his sister Klara who, when it came to the crisis, seems to have sided with Minna:

> For six long years it was the love of that young woman who kept me going and consoled and especially strengthened me to continue to live side by side with Minna, despite the enormous differences in our characters and our natures—this young woman who initially, and for a long time, only treated me with hesitation, doubt, reticence and shyness, but then approached me with increasing assurance and decisiveness. . . . From the very beginning of our acquaintance she cared for me unflaggingly and with the greatest sensitivity,

and whatever could ease the burden of my life she managed to obtain from her husband by her courage. . . . Her greatness lay in the fact that she always kept her husband informed of her emotions until, by and by, she could persuade him to accept the loss of her with resignation. It is easy to gauge what sacrifices and battles this must have cost. . . . Whilst he was devoured by jealousy, she always knew how to re-awaken his interest for me so that—as you know—he often supported me. When finally it came to my desire to own a small house with a garden, it was she who after severe strife talked him into buying for me the fine grounds adjoining their property. . . . This unbelievable success was achieved by the wondrous love of this purest, noblest of women. . . . But we both realized immediately that there could never be any thought of a union between us: we resigned ourselves to our fate, denying ourselves every egoistic desire; we suffered and endured, but—we loved each other!

At that time Wagner stood under the mighty influence of Schopenhauer's philosophy, and as complementary opposite to all this noble resignation it is also necessary to consider a portion of a letter to Mathilde, which will be quoted later (cf. p. 70) and which can hardly be misunderstood. In another letter to her Wagner shows how clearly he realized the bearing which his love had on his work: "From the very depth of my soul and in all eternity I must offer thanks to you that I could write *Tristan*."

There is no need to explain the autobiographical element in the relationship Tristan—Isolde—King Marke, and it is sheer idle speculation whether Wagner's passion was released by the artistic concept which was filling his innermost being, or whether to that passion must be ascribed the direct cause of the composition of *Tristan*. One thing is certain: he was passionately ablaze. It was Minna who precipitated the crisis when she intercepted a letter and provoked a violent scene. A further stay in the "haven" had become impossible because the local town gossips had smelt out the scandal. Minna was bundled off to take a cure on account of her weak heart, and Wagner retreated into solitude—to Venice—to complete his *Tristan*, the work

which occupied his mind to the exclusion of everything else.
Once again the external affairs of his life had been shaken to
their foundations: once again he was homeless—and was to
remain homeless for years.

When Wagner left his "haven", the first act of *Tristan* was
completed and the engraving of the score had already been
begun. On the strength of the great success of *Lohengrin*
Breitkopf & Härtel had acquired the opera for publication and
had agreed to pay the composer an advance for every act
delivered—an advance which Wagner needed badly. In
Venice, where he arrived towards the end of August 1858, he
found an apartment suited to his tastes in the Palazzo
Giustiniani on the Grand Canal. His life, as he describes it in
his letters, was of monastic isolation: completely devoted to his
work, which he only left in the evenings to take a gondola
across to St Mark's Square. Incidentally, the "monk" had
furnished his cell quite prettily, for he could never live without
comfort:

> I immediately strove to overcome the lack of elegance and
> comfort of my dwelling: I had the doors removed between
> an enormous bedroom and a small adjoining chamber, and
> had them replaced by curtains. They are not of such beautiful
> material as the last ones in the "haven"; for the time being
> cotton has to serve as *décor*, and this time it had to be red as
> the rest of the furnishings are of that colour, only the bedroom
> is green. . . .

His sole company was Karl Ritter, who had come with him to
Venice, but Ritter must not disturb him: he was only allowed
to pay Wagner a short visit in the evening or to accompany
him occasionally on his walks. In St Mark's Square the Austrian
military band often played his music. One disadvantage of his
renown was that one day he was summoned by the police, who
gave him a visitor's permit of only a few months' duration. It is
true that the Italian provinces of the Habsburg monarchy did
not belong to the German Confederation so that there was no
immediate danger for Wagner, but the Austrian officials
mistrusted this notorious revolutionary and did their best to rid
themselves of him with as good grace as possible.

It will not come as a surprise that once again he ran out of money, and this caused a profound disagreement between him and Liszt. Wagner considered that Liszt should provide him with what effectively amounted to a guaranteed annual income, no matter from what source, but this time Liszt, ever generous and prepared to help, had to disappoint him: he himself was in a critical stage of his career and had to give up his position in Weimar. At the same time he expressed his fervent admiration of the first act of *Tristan*, of which he had seen the proofs of the score, and Wagner made the most unkind comment that he would have preferred some money to all this admiration. (Like several others, this letter was suppressed in the first publication of their correspondence.) Fortunately some other unexpected emoluments came to hand, and in early March he could deliver the second act of *Tristan* to his publishers, which meant that another advance was due. At that time the clouds of the war between Austria and France (with its ally Sardinia) which was to break out in the following summer were already gathering. Add to this the gentle pressure exerted by Austrian officialdom, and it seemed advisable to leave Italy. Wagner completed the third act of *Tristan* in August in Lucerne. For a short while he stayed in Zürich with the Wesendoncks; as he writes himself, the main purpose of this visit was to counter the local gossip. In addition it had the result that Otto Wesendonck, with the completed sections of the *Ring* as surety, lent him 24,000 francs to go to Paris and do something for the promotion of his works. He knew very well that this loan would never be repaid, but apparently he considered the price cheap in order to get this brilliant but embarrassing man out of the way.

This time Wagner returned to Paris as a *grand seigneur*. Minna came to join him and together they took up residence in an elegant apartment, but it can be assumed that the marriage as such had by then ceased to exist. He went his own ways, and the "monastic isolation" had definitely come to an end. He booked an orchestra and gave three concerts in which he made the Parisian public acquainted with excerpts from his works. Artistically they were a tremendous success, financially a dead loss, and this deficit was increased even more when he followed some irresponsible advice to repeat those concerts in Brussels:

he always had a tendency to follow any advice that happened
to flatter his optimism. Still, he could find some more
sacrificially-minded enthusiasts, and he also succeeded in
selling *Das Rheingold* to Edition Schott, Mainz, for the sum of
10,000 francs. The Wesendonck loan he had forgotten with the
same rapidity with which he had spent the money. However,
the main purpose of his hopes he had not achieved: to find a
wealthy patron who would finance his bold plan to put on a
season of German opera in Paris, during which he would have
produced *Tannhäuser*, *Lohengrin* and *Tristan und Isolde* with
select German singers—and an artistically-minded friend, the
fiscal collector Lucy of Marseille, was very glad to get out of it
all for a mere down-payment of a few thousand francs. Wagner
now turned his attention to the *Opéra*, but the reception was
cool. He realized that only a peremptory order of Emperor
Napoleon III could help him and thought to find contacts in
diplomatic circles. Again he was lucky: Fürstin Metternich,
wife of the Austrian ambassador in Paris and an intimate friend
of Empress Eugénie, had the ear of the Emperor. In Dresden
she had heard *Tannhäuser* and admired Wagner and, to please
her, Napoleon ordered *Tannhäuser* to be performed at the
Opéra. Wagner now ruled the roost.

Much has been written about the three ill-fated *Tannhäuser*
performances in Paris in March 1861 which unleashed one of
the greatest theatrical scandals in the history of opera. Seen
from a little distance the main trouble seems to have been an
absurd collision between German and French sensibility, and
what happened then was a mere burlesque prelude to the
murderous tragedy of 1870. Initially there was every good will
to produce *Tannhäuser* with all the glitter and glamour which
the greatest opera house of the world could muster. All the
singers whom Wagner deemed essential were specially engaged,
the *décor* was as voluptuous and costly as he could wish, the
orchestra and the entire cast were at his unrestricted disposal
for months. His only complaint concerned the conductor, whom
he considered completely inadequate; and he could do nothing
about it. The most natural thing would have been to ask the
composer himself to conduct, but this was not permissible
according to the *règlement*. Hans von Bülow was in Paris at the

time, and he describes the *Opéra*'s conductor as a "despicable blockhead, an old man with no intelligence and no memory, completely incapable of learning a lesson. This was proved in the innumerable rehearsals, the purpose of which was basically so that *he* could learn the score." It is part and parcel of the burlesque that this conductor was Pierre Dietsch, the composer of *Le Vaisseau Fantôme* the libretto of which, twenty years earlier, had been tailored for him on the basis of Wagner's draft for the *Holländer*.

It was not merely the incompetence of the conductor which conjured up the catastrophe, but also the conflict of interests and attitudes for which no compromise could be found. Ballet was one of the traditional peculiarites of the Paris *Opéra*. It was considered an integral part of an opera performance, and traditionally the great ballet scene had to come in the second act, as High Society was accustomed to dine first and then make its appearance at the *Opéra* after 10 p.m. In his writings Berlioz tells us that the dancers were not paid: the fact that they danced in the opera ballet was regarded as a sort of sideline. Their patrons and supporters belonged to a large extent to the highest strata of the ruling aristocracy, and these *habitués* were most adamant that, when visiting the *Opéra*, they should not be cheated out of that part which was of preponderant interest to them. From the very outset it had been pointed out to Wagner again and again that a ballet in the second act was a *must*, but he had steadfastly refused Royer, director of the *Opéra*, any concessions along those lines. His counter-suggestion was to enlarge the opening scene of the first act by a ballet-pantomime on a lavish scale: "Whenever I talked to that man he came up with his admonition that there should be a ballet in the second act. I may have stunned him with my eloquence, but I never succeeded in convincing him." It always perturbed Wagner a good deal when his oratorical efforts misfired.

All in all the *Opéra* must have been an exceedingly cumbersome apparatus. During the summer of 1860 the French translation of the text had been achieved, and in connection with the *Bacchanale*—the new ballet episode for the beginning of the first act—Wagner had thoroughly re-worked the entire *Venusberg* scene as well as making some alterations in the

Sängerkrieg which had not satisfied him completely. The *Tannhäuser* rehearsals began in autumn and continued throughout the winter. Amongst those taking part it was not only the untalented conductor who was irritated by Wagner's arrogant manner: on such occasions tension and friction are unavoidable, and Wagner was not the most patient of producers. In this connection it must also be admitted that, although on artistic grounds Wagner's opposition to the inclusion of a second-act ballet is understandable, he would hardly have prejudiced the future of *Tannhäuser* if he had made a concession to the traditions of the institution: there is a great deal of ballet music in *Rienzi*, and he could easily have agreed that some of this music be used as an interlude in the Paris performance. His Italian contemporary Verdi, who had a much simpler and more broad-minded attitude in matters of the theatre, had always made such concessions to the Paris *Opéra*, and even in *Otello* he added some ballet music for the Paris performance without thereby losing one iota of his dignity. But Wagner's stubbornness was part and parcel of his character and his exceptional artistic personality; the fact that he had to suffer for it was a tragedy which was not particularly surprising for those who knew him.

The members of the posh and exclusive Jockey Club were all subscribers to the *Opéra* and could exert some decisive influence. From the very beginning they were the executive power of an opposition which was determined to create a furore which would make the *Tannhäuser* performance impossible. The hunting whistles which they had brought with them produced an argument which even the Wagnerian orchestra could not counter. The police were hesitant to take action, for the imperial régime treated the loyalistically-inclined aristocracy with kid gloves. The rumpus increased from performance to performance, and after the third Wagner withdrew his score. He had to write off one-and-half wasted years as a total loss, and the *Opéra* a not inconsiderable sum which they had spent on *Tannhäuser*.

However, the contacts with diplomatic circles which Wagner had made during that time led to a secondary result of some importance. Both Prussia and Austria had intervened discreetly and had succeeded in obtaining a concession from the Saxon government which earlier would have been completely out of the question: they gave an amnesty to Wagner and now, for the first time after twelve years of exile, he could set foot on German soil again.

5

NOMADIC YEARS
(1861–1864)

THE SUBSEQUENT YEARS of Wagner's life resembled a nightmare. He himself had become a "Flying Dutchman", tossed and turfed about without sense of direction, without peace and quiet, without a home. In his mind there were only two immutable aims to which he clung with that iron determination so characteristic of him: to get *Tristan* performed, and to find the time and equanimity to create a great new work. Two years had gone by since the completion of *Tristan*, two years of which the only artistic outcome had been the Paris revision of *Tannhäuser*. Then his creative genius possessed him again, and it is incomprehensible with what assurance he himself knew that once again the miracle of inspiration had happened within him, and that from this inspiration something great, something wonderful would result. Anyone but Wagner would have jealously concealed this as an intimate, personal secret, but in his extrovert manner he had to tell everyone to whom he happened to be writing. Perhaps Mathilde Wesendonck was the first to know about it when he asked her to return the old Dresden draft of the *Meistersinger* which he had left with her. In autumn 1861 he happened to be in Nürnberg—

... and suddenly I heard music which could be an overture to the *Meistersinger von Nürnberg*. When I had returned to my tavern in Vienna, I quickly worked out the entire plan in unbelievable haste. I felt very happy when I noticed that my memory had remained as clear as crystal, and that my imaginative fantasy was willing and abundant.

In the *Hofbibliothek* in Vienna Cornelius traced for him the principal historical source which he used as a basis: Johann

Christoph Wagenseil's *Buch von der Meistersinger holdseliger Kunst* ("The Book of the Mastersinger's Gracious Art") of 1697. In December he returned to Paris, and within the space of four weeks he completed the entire text for this new composition; while taking a walk he wrote down the melody of the *Wach auf* chorus which had suddenly come to him. To Mathilde he wrote: "My *Meistersinger* will dumbfound you!" (In his letters to Mathilde he had long abandoned the intimate Tristan-style of the Venice days and had reverted to the formal German *Sie* in addressing her.) "Keep a firm hold on your emotions when it comes to Sachs, or you will fall in love with him! It is a marvellous piece of work. The old draft had little or nothing to offer." And, being Wagner, he could not but add: "One simply must have experienced paradise to get to the true heart of such a matter." On his birthday, 22 May, he wrote to her:

> Suddenly I had an idea for the orchestral introduction to the third act of *Meistersinger*. This act will lead to a most dramatic climax when Sachs rises in front of the whole assembled populace and is received by them in an exultation of enthusiasm. Clearly and solemnly all the people sing the first eight lines of Sachs's poem to Luther. For this the music has been written. Now, as an introduction to the third act where, when the curtain rises, Sachs is sitting in a mood of deep meditation, I have a melody of great melancholy played by the lower instruments, softly and gently: it will have a character of utter resignation, when suddenly the horns and other mellifluous wind instruments play the solemn, yet joyously-bright tune of the *Wach auf* as though it were the gospel, which then blossoms forth in the whole orchestra. I have come to realize that this will be my masterpiece and—that I shall live to complete it.

And on the same day he wrote to his young friend Wendelin Weissheimer: "Since this morning, the early morning hours of my birthday, I know that *Die Meistersinger* will be my masterpiece."

But all this is anticipating future events. After the *Tannhäuser* scandal in Paris Wagner, who was at liberty to return to

Germany, had immediately tried most energetically to get
Tristan performed. To this end he had had Karlsruhe in view
for quite some time, because he knew that the Grossherzog of
Baden was favourably disposed towards him, and that
Tannhäuser and *Lohengrin* were in the repertoire of the *Hoftheater*.
Unfortunately Karlsruhe lacked the necessary singers for the
principal roles, and so Wagner went to Vienna in order to
conclude guest engagements with singers of his own choice on
behalf of the Karlsruhe *Hoftheater*. The Vienna *Hofkapellmeister* Esser, with whom Wagner had been in contact for quite
some time, invited him to hear a *Lohengrin* performance, and
there with indescribable emotion he heard his own work for the
first time:

> That *Lohengrin* performance which I attended was one of
> those continuous ovations which I have only experienced
> with Viennese audiences. They also wanted to perform for me
> my other two operas, but I felt a certain reticence and did
> not want a repetition of what I had experienced on this even-
> ing. In addition I had been informed of the great weaknesses
> of their staging of *Tannhäuser*, and so I only went to a perform-
> ance of *Der fliegende Holländer*, even though it was more
> modest, particularly as I wanted to get to know the singer
> Beck who was supposed to excel in that opera. Again the
> public was unboundedly enthusiastic and thus, carried on a
> wave of public approbation, I could now turn to my real
> business.

This, however, did not prove an easy matter. The *Intendant* in
Vienna could not be persuaded to give leave of absence to the
requisite singers to go to Karlsruhe, and it was suggested to
Wagner that the first performance of *Tristan* should take place
at the Vienna opera as they had the necessary vocal forces.
This proposal was accepted, and it was agreed that the
performance should take place during the next season—
1861–62.

Again there were complications. Frau Meyer-Dustmann,
whom Wagner had chosen for the role of Isolde, was both
willing and eager, but Alois Ander who was to sing Tristan had

chronic trouble with his voice, so that the rehearsals which had begun at the beginning of the season soon had to be interrupted. During this interim period Wagner re-visited Paris and wrote the text of the *Meistersinger*. Immediately afterwards he read this text to a group of friends in Mainz in the house of Schott, the publishers who had acquired the work. It is a typically Wagnerian trait that for this important occasion he commanded the presence of his Viennese friend Peter Cornelius—at Wagner's request another Viennese friend, Dr med. Stand-hartner, had to furnish the funds for Cornelius' travelling expenses—and it is equally charming to read his report to Mathilde:

On 5 February in Mainz in the house of Schott I first read the text to some friends. Unfortunately there was no chance of reading it to you first. But I had to have someone to replace you, and so before my departure from Paris I wrote to Cornelius in Vienna (about whom in the course of time you will hear much more) that he must be at Schott in Mainz by the evening of the fifth, otherwise I would again give him the formal *Sie* instead of the friendly *Du*. Now it was a case of Schiller's *Bürgschaft*: as you know, all rivers had burst their banks, many trains were not running, there was danger everywhere. No matter: on the dot of seven on the fifth my Cornelius arrived, and the following day he made the return journey to Vienna! But you must realize what a poor devil he is, how he has to eke out his living with giving lessons in order to make his forty florins per month. But—he idolizes me!

Wagner had succeeded in persuading his publisher to give him some advance for his *Meistersinger*, on the strength of which he settled in Biebrich near Mainz to work in peace. For the last time he attempted to cohabit with Minna, but the attempt only resulted in painful scenes. Their separation became inevitable and final, and she returned to Dresden. Wagner had promised her 1000 *Taler* per annum as alimony, and during the years to come he stuck to this promise as well as he could. For the rest his doctor and friend Pusinelli in Dresden had to

come to the rescue—Wagner owed him a lot of money ever
since his Dresden days in any case, so that a little more or less
did not matter.

Wagner's financial problems had become insoluble long ago.
In the days of the *Holländer* 500 francs were still of some help to
him; now a tenfold amount was only a drop in the bucket. It is
quite futile to attempt to total up the monies which he
squandered during the Paris years of the *Tannhäuser* adventure.
Being an eternal optimist, he always added amounts which he
was expecting to come in to the credit side of his ledger. Apart
from that he was utterly unscrupulous in his borrowings and
quite unconcernedly spent the last *Taler* of a friend for some
whim or other. In 1859 he had gone to Paris with the nice
little nest-egg which Wesendonck had provided, but just a few
months later he tried to get some more money from an old
friend in Dresden, the tenor Tichatschek:

> Next year I shall earn a lot with *Tristan* and, above all,
> *Tannhäuser* will prove itself in Paris, but for the moment I do
> not know what to do. So here I am, with the expectation of
> an assured income of more than 5000 francs in about spring
> of next year, which I would love to receive now in advance:
> it is the Vienna fee for *Tristan*. They are most eager to have
> the opera soon, but I cannot let them have it now before I
> have performed it myself. . . . Do you know anyone who
> could advance 5000 francs to me? After all that has gone
> before, should it really be so impossible to obtain this sum
> for me immediately—after all, it is not so exorbitant—on the
> security of such a certain income? As I am really in a bad
> and ever-increasing plight (for no one here must know
> anything about it) I enclose a deed of assignment which
> perhaps would suffice initially. For heaven's sake, do your
> best and see what a friend can do for a friend. . . . If the
> total loan cannot be realized at once, I could manage on
> half the amount for the time being, as long as I can count on
> the balance before the end of the year. But to have real
> peace of mind I would have to receive the entire amount at
> once.

In Biebrich he was once again in dire financial straits. So on 9 September 1862, he wrote to another singer, Ludwig Schnorr, who was singing Lohengrin and Tannhäuser in Karlsruhe:

> Now I offer you the opportunity to show to me by a great effort that you are my follower. You are in a position to help me, be it out of your own means or be it through your personal guarantee, and thereby finally to set my life on its necessary course. For my purposes I must have 1500 to 2000 *Taler*, of these at least 1000 *Taler* immediately.... Much depends on your reply.

A few months earlier he had written along similar lines to Countess Pourtalès, the wife of the Prussian Ambassador in Paris:

> Gracious friend, please do understand that it must be a noble cause which enables me to overcome my most understandable shyness and to ask you fervently if you could somehow make it possible to assist me quickly with a matter of 1200 *Taler*. I believe I am justified to presume that, once I have concluded the work which will probably occupy me to the exclusion of everything else for the rest of this year, I shall be in a position to repay this requested sum which, at the moment, I really need to regularize my situation. I would be overjoyed and honoured if you could let me have this money as a loan, and I assure you that such proof of friendship would have the inestimable value for me that it would enable me to dedicate myself entirely to my work.

As a matter of fact the Countess remitted to Wagner the amount he had asked for, but, as can be seen from the above, it did not last long.

Wendelin Weissheimer, pupil of Liszt and fanatical admirer of Wagner, has already been mentioned. He was conductor at the Mainz theatre when Wagner settled in Biebrich. His invaluable advantage was that he had a wealthy father, a fact out of which Wagner occasionally drew some profit. At the time of the letter to Schnorr cited above he also wrote to Weissheimer:

Things are not going well with me. From the enclosed letter [from Schott, who are refusing to pay any further advances] you will see how little I can rely on Schott. . . . I ask you, please have a long talk with your dear father. . . . If my situation is to be entirely stabilized once and for ever, I would need an unconditional loan of 5000 guilders. . . . I would place all my income from the various theatres—that is to say all fees or royalties payable to me by the theatre managements for my opera *Die Meistersinger* (with the sole exception of the Berlin royalties)—at the entire disposal of your father until such time as the loan plus accrued interest has been repaid. I am firmly convinced that in this manner the debt would be completely cleared by the New Year of 1864. . . . Do try to persuade your dear father!

It proved an abortive attempt. Wagner's calculations had also been over-optimistic, for he only completed *Meistersinger* in 1867. From that period of insolvency Weissheimer also quotes a remark of Wagner's: "Truly, I am in such a position that, if somebody should make me an offer, I would be prepared to sell my immortality for 5000 guilders." But somehow or other he always managed to scrape together some money from somewhere. Von Bülow who, with his young wife Cosima (a daughter of Liszt's) had visited Wagner in Biebrich, wrote to Weissheimer: ". . .It is incredible how much money can be spent in a fortnight." And he added: "It is a riddle to me how he always knows how to get hold of the necessary when it is absolutely essential to him—perhaps he is an even greater genius in matters of finance than he is as a poet and composer."

Weissheimer was enterprising. He wanted to give a concert in Leipzig in order to make himself known as a conductor and composer, and so he suggested to Wagner that the Prelude to *Die Meistersinger*, which Wagner had completed during the spring in Biebrich, should be performed on this occasion. This work and the *Tannhäuser* Overture were conducted by Wagner himself, von Bülow played a Liszt piano concerto, and the rest of the programme consisted of Weissheimer's own compositions. Financially the venture was a dead loss: few people were in the audience, and father Weissheimer lost a lot of money. But Wagner's music aroused much enthusiasm, and the *Meistersinger* Prelude had to be encored. It would appear that at that time a deep affection between Wagner and Cosima von Bülow was already burgeoning.

During the restive Biebrich period the composition of *Die Meistersinger* progressed but haltingly, and Wagner came to a dead stop in the middle of the first act. He then gave up his Biebrich residence and returned to Vienna in the middle of November in order to overcome the doldrums in which *Tristan* lay. The difficulties were still the same: Alois Ander was obviously afraid of the physical demands of the role, and another Tristan was not to be found. A further difficulty was precipitated by Wagner himself. In Biebrich a very pretty girl from Mainz, Mathilde Maier, had helped to console him. To Vienna he brought her namesake, Friederike Meyer, an actress of the Frankfurt theatre whom he had enticed away from the director of that theatre, and now, quite unconcernedly, he introduced her as his paramour. Peter Cornelius tells about it all in the critically observant manner which is so typical of him:

We had a musical soirée for his Fräulein Friederike Meyer. Her chambermaid also sat in the room as a sort of duenna. Things are not as bad with Friederike as Mainz tries to make us believe: she appears to be quite a nice girl. She is sensible and does not want to play to the gallery. One could not call her pretty, but she has a lively personality. Wagner behaved very nicely and with decorum in her company. If he has to have such affairs I should think that with this one he is doing quite well.

There was only one snag: Friederike was the sister of Frau Dustmann who studied the part of Isolde and until then had been Wagner's most reliable ally in the *Tristan* business. She considered his behaviour with her sister a public scandal, and so ended a beautiful friendship.

Wagner felt like making music again, so he repeated his Paris experiment and gave three concerts in Vienna with excerpts from his latest works: *Das Rheingold, Die Walküre, Siegfried, Die Meistersinger*. From the last-named he selected Pogner's great scene—this was the point he had just reached in the composition. His earlier works had long been popular in Vienna, and he wanted to save up *Tristan* for the imminent production at the *Hofoperntheater*. Artistically he scored a magnificent success, but the financial deficit was again anything but negligible. He then accepted an invitation to Prague, and in February he went to Russia where he conducted concerts in St Petersburg and Moscow and was celebrated everywhere. But the financial result was much smaller than he had expected, and also he had absented himself from Vienna at a decisive moment—just then Schnorr, who had already studied the part of Tristan, would have been available for a guest engagement— and spoilt his last chances of a performance: *Tristan* was dropped and postponed for an indefinite period.

From his Russian trip Wagner had brought back 4000 *Taler* to Vienna—much less than he had hoped for, but still a tidy little sum—and now he fixed himself up in a comfortable country house in the suburb of Penzing complete with two servants, a gardener and a pretty chambermaid. To this latter he once even wrote a love letter which, by an indiscreet accident, has been preserved. (The Friederike Meyer affair was already over.) During the summer he conducted two concerts in Budapest, and during the following autumn and winter quite a few concerts in Prague, Karlsruhe, Breslau. But this was the dilemma: his strenuous conducting activity took away all the energies he needed for composing, and *Die Meistersinger* did not get ahead. As he wrote to Weissheimer on 10 July 1863:

I cannot go on like this, and I feel a stranger in this world in which I am bound hand and foot—be it for art and life, for aspiration and emotion. Nothing pleases me any more: all these upheavals and my recognition of the impotence of the individual are too great and too decisive. At your age you may find it difficult to understand this. As far as I am concerned I can express it quite simply—I am fed up with life! What I lack is no less than *everything* in order to live as a civilized human being. . . . Lately I have been working again on the orchestration of *Meistersinger*, but it is progressing very slowly. I must confess that the abundant spring of humour and high spirits from which the joy of this kind of work should flow has dried up completely within myself.

On the whole he had a very pleasant life in Penzing. He always had a great need of stimulating company, and this was amply provided by Peter Cornelius and his friend Carl Tausig (who also stemmed from the Weimar circle around Liszt), the physician and musical enthusiast Dr Standhartner, as well as the Prague musician Heinrich Porges who later proved to be of invaluable service as a propagandist. All this would have been fine if it had not been for the nightmare of his debts which had grown terrifyingly. He was continuously reminded of the monies he owed for the costly furnishings of his new dwelling. It was the same story as once upon a time in Dresden: he had to make a new hole in order to plug up the old one and had to take up short-term credits at usurious rates of interest. As for his Viennese friends, what they could do for him was strictly limited. He had been confident of being again engaged for concerts in Russia, but this hope proved to be ephemeral. In the early months of the new year 1864 his position was nothing short of desperate. He thought of suicide and, as he wrote himself, he composed "a humorous epitaph" for himself. Legal measures were invoked, and once again there was the threat of the debtors' prison. His friend Dr Standhartner advised him to flee and provided him with the necessary funds. At dead of night his personal belongings were got out of the house; at dead of night he left Vienna. Once again he was a fugitive as he had been many years ago—then from Riga, from Dresden; now from Vienna.

He went to Zürich where he thought he had the best chance of finding friends and assistance, and Frau Eliza Wille in Mariafeld near Zürich gave him hospitality. He stayed with her for a few weeks—and sleepless nights—in great worry about his affairs in Vienna where they had sold all his furniture in order to cover the most urgent debts. Carl Tausig was on a concert tour at the time and could not return to Vienna, because he had stood guarantor for Wagner and was now in danger of being arrested himself. Otto Wesendonck was unapproachable, but he offered Wagner some pocket-money for the duration of his stay in Zürich: a matter of 100 francs per month, which Wagner rejected with indignation. On 30 April he moved on to Stuttgart, where he had a devoted friend in the newly appointed *Hofkapellmeister* Karl Eckert, the former director of the Vienna Opera, who now was supposed to find a refuge for him somewhere in the vicinity. All Wagner's actions during this time of crisis were characterized by the state of panic of one who is nearly out of his mind. He sent a telegram to Wendelin Weissheimer: "I am at the end of my tether—I cannot go on—somehow I must vanish out of this world. Can you not preserve me?" And Wendelin, whose father obviously had buttoned up his pockets in matters concerning Wagner, immediately came to Stuttgart to be by the side of his harassed friend and to accompany him wherever. "He could not be left alone in this situation. Soon we made up our minds and agreed on some isolated spot in the Rauhe Alb."

Wagner covered up his tracks as best he could and was therefore most embarrassed when suddenly an unknown visitor was announced. Weissheimer, who had just been with Wagner to help him pack his trunks, left him alone with this visitor.

When finally this gentleman [Pfistermeister, Cabinet Secretary to the King of Bavaria] had taken his leave and I could rejoin Wagner, I found him completely overcome by this unexpected turn in his fortunes: he showed me a precious diamond ring and, on the table, a wonderful photographic portrait of the King. Then, beside himself with joy, he burst into tears and embraced me with the words: "That *this* should happen—and happen just at this moment!"

What had happened can be told in a few words. As a result of the sudden death of the Bavarian King Maximilian II, his eighteen-year-old son Ludwig II had acceded to the throne. In his earliest youth Wagner's *Lohengrin* had impressed him indelibly. A few years later he had heard this work again in

Munich as well as *Tannhäuser*. As a result he had studied
Wagner's writings, including the texts of his stage-works, and
had fallen a slave to his romanticism and the whole world of his
ideas. After only several weeks on the throne, he ordered his
Cabinet Secretary Franz von Pfistermeister to trace Wagner
and summon him to his presence. Pfistermeister had started on
his journeys on 14 April, had first sought Wagner in Penzing
and then, after laborious researches at Frau Wille's in Mariafeld.
But Wagner had just left, and finally he tracked him down in
Stuttgart on 3 May. On the very same day he accompanied
him to Munich. A letter to Weissheimer (20 May 1864) gives
us detailed information about all the circumstances as well as
Wagner's own reactions:

Just two little words to confirm to you the indescribable good
fortune which has become my lot. Everything has happened
in a way which is beyond the most beautiful of dreams.
Through the love of the young King I am now protected
against every care for all times: I can work, I do not have to
worry about anything—and I have no title, no official
position and no responsibility of any kind. If I want to
perform any work of mine the King will place everything I
may need at my disposal. . . . For me this young King is the
most wonderful gift of the Fates. We love each other as only
master and disciple can love one another. He is blissfully
happy to have me, as I am to have him. He has educated his
mind entirely from my works and writings, and in his
entourage he openly admits that I am his only real tutor. At
that he is so beautiful and profound that the now daily
meetings with him are exciting and stimulate me to a new
life.

You can imagine how much envy I have to face. My
influence on the young monarch is so great that all those who
do not know me are deeply concerned. For this reason the
large salary which the King has granted me is quoted as less
than it really is. I myself—as this also corresponds to my
nature and inclination—keep completely in the background
and try to soothe everyone so that, by and by, their fears may
be allayed. I can already twist Lachner [the musical director

of the Munich Opera] round my little finger. Like myself, the King despises the theatre. We are just letting things go their way and are biding our time, until in a suitable manner we can channel them in a more noble direction.

On the same day he also wrote to Ludwig Schnorr:

A young king, intelligent, profound and unbelievably sincere who quite openly, in front of everyone, calls me his one and only tutor! He knows my works and writings as perhaps no-one else, he is my pupil as perhaps no other, and he feels that it is his vocation to realize every one of my plans which can in any way be realized by human endeavour. And he is a king: he stands under no tutelage, under no influence, and he dedicates himself with such earnestness and assurance to the matters of state that all know and feel that he is a true king. . . .

Wagner's memoirs which, six years later, he dictated to Frau Cosima come to a conclusion on this decisive turn in his destiny with the following words:

On the same day I had received news from Vienna, advising me most emphatically that I should not return there. Such terrors were never again to recur in my life. The perilous path on which that day my destiny had called me to the highest goals was never to be free of cares and worries, some of them of a kind which at that time were quite unknown to me; however, under the protection of my regal friend I was never again to be oppressed by the burden of life's trivial pressures.

6

THE PRIDE AND THE GLORY

(1864–1883)

In the life of no artist is there a similar instance of a higher power intervening, of such a miraculous salvation from apparently inescapable ruin. The most incredible facet of the matter is that it was, in actual fact, Wagner himself who had given the cue to his saving *Deus ex machina*. When, at his own expense, he had published the text of his *Ring* two years earlier, he had added an epilogue in which he had discussed all the difficulties to be overcome if the staging of this monumental work should ever become a practical reality. He was well aware of these difficulties; they were the reason why he lost courage in the middle of *Siegfried* and had given up the composition. The epilogue ends as follows:

I can see only two ways:

A large number of art-loving men and women who get together in the first instance to raise the necessary funds for a first performance of my work. When I consider the narrow-minded attitude of the average German towards such schemes I do not have the courage to hope for much success from the sort of appeal which would have to be launched for the purpose.

It would be much easier for some German monarch, for it need not be a new item in his budget: he could simply utilize those funds which up to now have been granted for the upkeep of the worst of public art institutions—that opera theatre which has for long so utterly lowered and degraded the German taste for music. If in his residence those visiting the opera evening after evening were insistent that the distracting tonic of modern opera must continue, the monarch of my imagination would have to allow this entertainment to go on—but not at his expense. Let him believe what he may: with his financial generosity towards his theatre he has patronized neither music nor drama, but solely the sort of opera which is nothing but an insult to the German sense of music and drama.

I would first have to demonstrate to him that he would be in a position of exerting an enormous influence on the morality of an artistic *genre* which until now has been debased, and of making possible the creation of characteristically German works. From his annual budget he would merely have to set aside the amount which hitherto had been spent on the upkeep of opera in his residence. This amount would then be devoted to repeated festival performances of the type as outlined—yearly, if the sum were sufficient, else every two or three years as the requisite funds had accumulated. He could thus institute a foundation which would give him incalculable influence on the development of German art, on the formation of a true national spirit free from arrogance; and for his own name he would gain immortal glory.

Can such a prince be found?

"In the beginning was the deed."

The young enthusiast, now on the throne, had read these words and considered that they applied to him. His first independent act of government was to put his decision into effect, to summon the object of his reverence to him and to help him in the realization of his plans. Wagner had succeeded in achieving that which, in the most precise terms, he had set himself as his aim. It would hardly be an exaggeration to say that Wagner had created for himself the King Ludwig which he needed.

As after the storms of the Dresden revolution, it was a long time after the ravages of this most terrible crisis of his life before he could regain his inner equilibrium. As ever, his creative output is the most reliable indicator of his condition: almost two years had to pass before he could take up his creative work with his old intensity. Many of the disastrous occurrences of those years can only be explained by the chronic unrest within himself. But probably the most important circumstance, as earlier in that weird existence, is the fact that he was quite incapable of living in peace with the world in general. He could never achieve a state of calm moderation because his implacability and his passionate manner of involving himself in each and every situation inevitably led to conflicts. For the first time he was completely independent artistically and materially, and he had the prospect that it would remain like this for the rest of his life. But it seems that in due course even those modest obligations which the unlimited love and admiration of King Ludwig imposed on him became too onerous, and very soon he began to misuse his influence over the young monarch—an influence which he was not disposed to share with anyone—with total unconcern.

His association with his royal friend began in the high spirits of a honeymoon. Ludwig resided in Schloss Berg on Lake Starnberg, Wagner in a villa nearby. As he wrote to Frau Wille:

> By carriage it takes me ten minutes to get there. Daily he sends for me once or twice, and I fly to him as to a beloved. It is a fascinating relationship. I have never before experienced such a wonderful, unrestrained urge for knowledge, such comprehension, such glowing fervency. And then the kindly way in which he takes care of me, this endearing purity of heart, and his countenance when he assures me how happy he is to have me. Thus we often sit for hours, gazing at each other and lost to the world.

Such a state of affairs could not last for long. Above all Wagner could not stand solitude; he wanted friends around him, and he had the need to share his happiness with others—that is to say "share" in the sense in which he understood that word. From his letter to Peter Cornelius of 23 May:

> I have told you repeatedly that I have carefully prepared everything here for your arrival. We two, and whoever else there may be, can live side by side completely independent of each other, each following his own task, his own mood, and still it is possible at any given moment to enjoy each other's

company. Your grand piano, which does not bother me, is standing there for you, a well-stocked box of cigars awaits you in your room, etc. Proof, dear Peter, of my eagerness!

Later he continues with some signs of irritation: "This letter demands a reply or—it will be revoked." In actual fact Cornelius was afraid of Wagner, as he felt he could not stand up to him—he was afraid that Wagner would take complete possession of him, and he was working on an opera. Much though he venerated and admired Wagner, he also wanted to preserve his personal freedom and his artistic integrity. This is what Wagner referred to in the following:

You have never replied to all my notes with even one single line, but through Heinrich Porges you let me know you were sorry that you could not come: that you had set yourself the aim of revising your *Cid* within the next three months and would have to stay in Vienna to do so.

Which is more advisable, dear Peter: shall we talk about this peculiar behaviour, or shall we be silent about it? . . . Either you accept my invitation without further delay and settle with me for just about the rest of your life in a truly homely union, or—you turn me down and expressly forgo my wish to have you live with me. In this latter case I also renounce you completely and utterly and shall arrange my own life without considering you in any way.

This is termed clapping the pistol to a man's head! But Cornelius resisted valiantly and stuck to his *Cid*. In the end Wagner must have understood his reasons and left him in peace. A few months later he had a new proposition for this friend whom he truly loved and whose stimulating company he valued (7 October 1864):

At the express demand of His Majesty King Ludwig II of Bavaria I am to request you to move to Munich as soon as you can; here you are to live solely for your art, ready to fulfil any special requests of the King, in order to help me, your friend, as a friend. From the day of your arrival you will receive an annual salary of 1000 guilders out of the Cabinet Purse of His Majesty.

Several days later Peter accepted, overjoyed—for in Vienna he had to earn his living miserably by badly-paid music lessons. Wagner replied:

I am grateful to you that you will come. You may regard your call to Munich in very simple terms. My gracious King, whose beauty and magnificence you simply cannot imagine, was happy to grant me everything which I need to complete my works. . . . But I cannot stand being alone. In summer I asked to have von Bülow, and he will be settling here next month with his wife and children. Now I still need you; I asked him for this favour, and you should have seen the joy with which this heavenly youth immediately commanded me to call you.

Bülow's duties in Munich consisted of playing for the King whenever required and of helping him to further his somewhat deficient musical education. However, this call to Munich which liberated von Bülow from the burden of his laborious, badly-paid activities as a piano teacher at the Stern Conservatorium in Berlin, was related to certain earlier events of which probably he knew nothing himself. When Peter had turned him down and his Mainz friend Mathilde Maier had also declined, Wagner had invited von Bülow and his family to spend the summer with him in Starnberg. Work detained Bülow for one week longer in Berlin than he had expected, and so he sent his wife Cosima with their two daughters, Daniela and Blandine, on ahead. They arrived in Starnberg on June 29, and what happened then may have been but the outcome of a development which had germinated for some time. Wagner always regarded Cosima's third daughter Isolde, born on 10 April of the following year, as his child. Much of this murky affair is a matter for speculation, as it is not certain when exactly von Bülow was informed about those facts which, one year later, were the talk of the town in Munich. Be that as it may, Wagner's next move was to push von Bülow's appointment as court pianist. Von Bülow with his family duly settled in Munich in November. From this time onwards Frau Cosima supervised the household in the opulent *palais* in the Briener Strasse which the King had rented for Wagner and later gave him as a present. She also looked after his correspondence and generally took off his shoulders as much of the burden of his everyday chores as she possibly could.

Although personal motives were predominant in the appointments of von Bülow and Cornelius, Wagner nevertheless also had his important, practical, matter-of-fact reasons. One of the main objects of his various reform plans for Munich was the foundation of a "German School of Music" which was to replace the existing Munich Conservatorium. He had already submitted a written memorandum to the King regarding the purpose and organization of this school. When later it actually came into existence, both friends played a leading role, as did Heinrich Porges and another friend and helper, the Leipzig singing teacher Friedrich Schmitt, whom Wagner also brought to Munich. As with all his theatrical plans, he had an eye to his own main chance in planning this music school: he wanted a training ground for singers for the peculiar vocal, musical and dramatic needs of his own works.

Cornelius's letters and diary entries throw quite a few sidelights on the situation in Munich and the then existing hothouse atmosphere:

Where Richard actually should worship, he enjoys and gorges himself. No chance of getting any work done!— Ludwig, who is young, inexperienced and enthusiastic, still seems to plunge head over heels into everything which will bring him into conflict with the world around him. . . .

My whole life here depends on the continuation of the ardent relationship of these two personalities. It is almost like a spiritual love affair and, like every couple of this sort, they are at loggerheads with the surrounding world and its precise, prosaic questions.

My own relationship to Wagner is untenable vis-à-vis this world, and my own self is also being destroyed. Wagner does not know or understand how exhausting he is—with this eternal sultriness, this languishing ever since the "accursed potion". Just as an example: the other day we were together with Frau von Bülow. Wagner took out Schack's *Firdusi* and started reading out a number of stanzas about Rostem and Suhrab. Meanwhile Bülow finished giving his lesson—not more than twelve minutes passed—we were in the middle of *Tristan und Isolde*—they sang the whole of the first act. Meanwhile tea was served—we had hardly drunk half a cup, and Wagner was completely involved telling us about his *Parsifal*—and this went on all evening until we parted. . . . Our great friend simply must talk, read, sing of himself, otherwise he is not content. That is the reason why he is ever avid for his own intimate circle, because it does not work out with other people. From the moment I dine with him—two o'clock in the afternoon—there is no getting away any more, or only very rarely. It is a state of affairs which nearly kills me.

It is obvious that he knew very well what a danger this great, irresistible, tyrannical friend was for him. It is an unfortunate fact that for Peter Cornelius, the creative artist, the meeting with Wagner was also his doom. He was only in his early thirties when he wrote his finest and most characteristic work—at a time before he became prisoner to that personality from which he could never free himself again. *Der Barbier von Bagdad* has remained his masterpiece. At the one and only performance of the *Barbier* in Weimar in 1858, the fiasco was due to a rowdy demonstration directed against the conductor, Liszt, who in consequence resigned on the spot. Cornelius was a delicate, sensitive artist, not at all equipped to fight the battles of this world, and this failure paralysed the wings of his inspiration. Under those circumstances the Wagnerian narcotic was poison for him. As far as originality and vigour is concerned, neither *Der Cid* nor *Gunlöd* (his unfinished third opera) can touch the *Barbier*—the only important and truly vital work to come forth from the Weimar circle. At the height of his powers Wagner need only have said one word in order to vindicate his friend's masterpiece by a repeat performance. Wagner did not say this word, and he never lifted one little finger in order to help this artist—about whose abilities he had no doubt—in the only way which would have counted: by encouraging his creative art. The *Barbier* reaped its belated laurels in Munich in 1885, but by then both Cornelius and Wagner lay under the green turf.

There can be no doubt that the hothouse climate surrounding Wagner must also have been disastrous for the young Ludwig who, in any case, was prone to eccentric over-excitement. The utter lack of concern with which Wagner used the Royal Favours for his own purposes unavoidably also led to difficulties. Amongst the upper classes of Munich—the court, ministry, high society interested in music and theatre—Wagner's appearance as the King's favourite, and all that went with it, must have caused a reaction in comparison with which a stirred-up hornets' nest would have been a mere triviality. The King paid Wagner's debts, his luxurious residence with its even more luxurious furnishings, as well as for the appointments of Wagner's friends to positions which were obvious sinecures, out of his private purse, but this did not stop people from doing their own calculations, and in their imagination the sums, which were sizeable anyway, were bloated still further. In addition Wagner's arrogance left nothing to be desired, and very soon his relationship with von Pfistermeister's Cabinet Chancellery became strained because of his uninhibited financial impositions. At the theatre ("I can twist Lachner round my little finger") Wagner's ruthless demands also made it difficult to maintain a state of peaceful co-operation. During the gala performances of *Der fliegende Holländer* and *Tannhäuser* (the first to be performed under the Wagner aegis) it was still a path strewn with roses, but when it came to the preparations for *Tristan und Isolde* and Hans von Bülow (meanwhile appointed "*Hofkapellmeister* for special duties") took charge, the first difficulties arose—for von Bülow had never been renowned for his patience or his excessive tact. He even got involved in a press campaign when he used a certain word not normally heard in polite society; it aroused a general feeling of animosity and endangered his position in Munich. He had considered it necessary to sacrifice the first row of the stalls in order to enlarge the orchestra pit, and during the discussions was rash enough to utter the rhetorical question whether it mattered very much if there were "thirty skunks more or less" in the theatre. Later he made some lame excuses, but he could not undo the "skunks". As von Bülow was a dyed-in-the-wool Prussian, his remark had the result that the entire Bavarian press was out for his blood. The most malicious insinuations against him began when Wagner's and Cosima's indiscretions were first noised abroad. So he became the first vulnerable victim of attacks which were actually directed against the "Master".

All the preparations for the *Tristan* performance stood under a strangely unlucky star. Wagner had engaged the Schnorrs to take the parts of Tristan and Isolde, and during the rehearsals they justified his confidence in them completely. Nor could he have found a better conductor than Hans von Bülow, who at one time had prepared the piano arrangement of the entire work and knew it inside out. Wagner could therefore concentrate on the production to the exclusion of everything else and achieve an overall effect of rare perfection. The first performance had been scheduled for 15 May 1865, but unfortunately a serious vocal indisposition of Malvine Schnorr compelled a postponement at the last moment. It finally took place on 10 June and became a furore. *Tristan und Isolde* was performed no less than four times up to 1 July, and each time it was greeted with enthusiasm. Then, only three weeks later, came the news of the sudden decease of Ludwig Schnorr. It is not surprising that the terror of the murderous physical demands made on the singers of the two title roles—a terror which had spread ever since the Viennese mishaps—was now increased. It is a fact that *Tristan* was the only one of Wagner's works which for a long time could not find its rightful place in the general repertoire of opera houses (always excepting *Parsifal*, which Wagner in his testament reserved for Bayreuth). When the news of Schnorr's death reached him, Wagner was literally shattered. He wrote to Pusinelli: "*Tristan* shall never be performed again. That will be my monument to this great singer." Such gestures of Wagner's are always magnificent; but he must have known that he did not mean it seriously, and that you cannot raise a monument to anyone by non-performances. . . .

Equally significant was his lack of concern when it came to other persons' feelings. He was most annoyed that Otto and

Mathilde Wesendonck did not attend the *première* of *Tristan* to which he had invited them. He wrote to Eliza Wille, who also had numbered amongst the absentees: "You all seem so small-minded to me, all of you who dodged this great excitement!" The fact that it might have been a trifle embarrassing for Mathilde and Otto to see themselves represented on the stage as Isolde and King Marke, and that perhaps some fingers might even be pointed at them, of course never entered his mind.

Poor Peter Cornelius provided another source of boundless irritation, for instead of attending the great *Tristan* event he had gone to Weimar to be present at the *première* of his own *Cid*—and it will be remembered that on one earlier occasion he had roused Wagner's ire with that particular work. Wagner really must have been beside himself with rage when, in an epistle dated 20 June 1865, he virtually threatened the very livelihood of his friend:

> Dear Cornelius, I must point out to you that you should make a petition to the King of Bavaria, informing him that you are leaving Munich and will in future no longer draw your salary. In my opinion you should simply refer to the turn of your fortunes which is keeping you outside Munich and makes your return impossible. If you do not inform me by 1 July that you have approached the King along these lines, I shall take it that you wish me to inform the King in your name, which I shall do on the date stated above.

We do not know Peter's reply to this ultimatum, but once again their differences were settled amicably.

Many things would not have happened in those days if Wagner had had only a modicum of feeling for the way in which, with his behaviour, he hurt the sensitivities of others. A prank which was played on him is quite symptomatic: he had asked the King for a special gift of 40,000 guilders to enable him to repay certain debts which were still outstanding. The King granted the request, and Frau Cosima went to the royal treasury to collect the money on his behalf—which she received in silver guilders. She had to hire two hackney-carriages in order to transport the heavy money-bags! But this was only a harmless jest in comparison with the ominous clouds which were gathering ever more threateningly above his head. Cornelius foresaw the approaching danger when he wrote to his fiancée:

> I have never mentioned it to you before, but Wagner has now entered into a political relationship with the King and has become a sort of Marquis Posa. . . . As an example, Wagner's friend Fröbel, a man of letters from Vienna, is to become editor of the official *Bayrische Zeitung*. . . . When Bülow first told me about this move—and you are the only person I take into my confidence—I shuddered, for here I saw the beginning of the end. A clash is absolutely inevitable when an artist tries to exert a decisive influence on the political life of a state. . . . An old adage comes to mind: "Cobbler, stick to your last!"—and in the case of Wagner, with reference to *Die Meistersinger* which he is composing for Schott, it could be twisted into: "Poet, stick to your cobbling!"

To Wagner's mind a music school had the single purpose of training Wagnerian singers, and a theatre of performing his works. In the same way he considered all ministers, politicians and cabinet secretaries useless if they were reluctant to further his own plans with all their energies. He tried to influence Ludwig against Pfistermeister who proved insufficiently pliable in his hands, and he never ceased his intrigues against *Ministerpräsident* Von der Pfordten who, from the very beginning, had quite openly opposed Wagner. The press was full of tirades against Wagner, which he ascribed to the Cabinet Chancellery and eventually he virtually demanded of the King the dismissal of the hated Pfistermeister as well as of Von der Pfordten. He even wrote an anonymous article in the *Neueste Nachrichten* in which he spoke of "two or three persons" whose removal was most desirable in the public interest. At this Von der Pfordten lost his patience and urged the King to get rid of Wagner, whose continued presence in Munich constituted a danger for the relationship between the King and his people and also for public safety. From Pfistermeister the King received a petition

with 4000 signatures which stated that the peace of the nation
was at peril, and Prince Karl von Bayern, Ludwig's uncle,
intervened in the name of the royal family. Ludwig had to
give in and ask his friend to leave Munich for some months. By
8 December 1865 the whole German press carried the news that
"by order of the King Herr Richard Wagner would have to
leave Bavaria, initially for several months". On the morning of
10 December he left Munich. Once again he had played for
high stakes and had lost.

Disillusioned and deflated, Wagner searched for a new
"haven", but he had succeeded in maintaining his independence, for he had ample funds in hand. Ludwig had been
compelled to give in to an irresistible pressure, but his love for
the great artist had remained unshaken and the flow of his
generous salary was not interrupted. Wagner's own emotions
as regards his benefactor were much more complex. From all
his utterances it is clear that he had the highest opinion of the
intelligence and talents of the young monarch, but he never
forgave him for the weakness he had shown on this occasion,
and also in years to come many of his actions bear witness to a
defiant, unfriendly attitude. Nevertheless from that time
onwards he made no further attempts to meddle directly in
Bavarian politics and became more cautious when giving
advice. Only in one respect did he never lack determination:
he was always decisively opposed whenever the King—who
ever-increasingly shunned all public appearances—spoke of
abdication. Of course, in this matter he also saw the danger to
his personal existence.

Wagner looked for a suitable spot where he could find peace
and seclusion. He tried Lake Geneva, then the South of France,
and finally found the right place on Lake Lucerne, not far from
Lucerne itself: the uninhabited and somewhat ramshackle
Villa Triebschen. He had it thoroughly renovated, and by the
spring it was fit to be lived in. With her three children Cosima
joined him there to make a snug home for him, and from that
time onwards she never left him. Earlier that year Minna had
died of her old heart complaint, and so at least from that direction
there was no legal obstacle to Wagner's union with the woman
he loved. Cosima's position was far more complicated for both

personal and public reasons. In Munich von Bülow was of the greatest possible importance for Wagner, and a public scandal had to be avoided at all cost, but it simply lay in the nature of things that this situation could never remain tenable for any length of time.

Wagner's seven Triebschen years can be considered as the happiest, most peaceful interlude of his whole life. He was free of the unrest, worries and intrigues of Munich; he could dedicate himself completely to his work, and he lived in beautiful surroundings with the woman of his choice in a domesticity arranged entirely in accordance with his own personal whims and requirements. By now he was fifty-three, of robust health and vitality, serenely self-assured of his sovereign artistic creativity. In Munich he had only worked on the *Siegfried* score, the second act of which had been left in abeyance as a sketch in 1858, and even this rather technical task had only progressed haltingly. His own instinct had kept him away from the work which needed his utter and undivided attention, and to which he could now turn at long last: *Die Meistersinger von Nürnberg. Die Meistersinger* was to be the first mature yield of this happy harvesting time.

The storms of the world at large did not make themselves very much felt on the placid shores of Lake Lucerne. Ludwig paid him a brief visit, for he insisted on coming in person to wish his beloved friend well on his birthday. Travelling incognito he arrived in Lucerne on 22 May. By doing so he re-confirmed his unshakeable faith in Wagner—and was the cause of a renewed press campaign against them both, for obviously knowledge of this visit soon became common property. The Prusso-Austrian conflict was then about to break out into open hostility, Bavaria being engaged on the Austrian side, and so the King's visit came near to being interpreted as high treason. However, the unfortunate outcome of this war (which cost Bavaria a large sum in reparations) also brought about a change in the ministry: Von der Pfordten had to go. Despite the insistence of the King, Wagner categorically refused to return to Bavaria, but at least the long-hoped-for Munich music school was opened with von Bülow as director. Another cherished plan of Wagner's was also realized with the creation of a newspaper. At his recommendation the Vienna publicist Julius Fröbel was engaged as editor of this new publication, the *Süddeutsche Presse*; he received a royal subsidy and agreed to the condition that Wagner would be in sole charge of the artistic supplement. In this supplement Wagner published a series of anonymous contributions which later were issued as a book with the title *Deutsche Kunst und deutsche Politik* ("German Art and German Politics"). The *Süddeutsche Presse* brought out twelve essays; the thirteenth was suppressed by Fröbel at the command of the King, as Wagner had once again dared go too far into political polemics, and this the King considered "suicidal". Wagner was most incensed and protested—without success. This incident was the partial cause of a cooling in the affections of the King for his rebellious protégé. But a much more serious reason was the fact that Wagner and Cosima made the King a sworn abettor of a lie: assuring him of their total innocence they persuaded him to sign a lengthy "declaration of honour" which Wagner himself had drawn up and which was to put an end to the defamations in the Munich press. The declaration misfired, and the only result was that the King was compromised as having attempted to cover up a shady affair which had been the subject of a public scandal.

By now—autumn 1867—the *Meistersinger* score had been completed, and because of *Meistersinger* a new young adept had joined Wagner who, in the future, was to belong to the inner-most circle of his helpers. His name was Hans Richter. He was a young musician, a horn player in the Vienna opera orchestra, whom Wagner took into his house. Sheet after sheet, as Wagner finished them, he had to make a copy of the score, and soon after rehearsals started for the *première* in Munich under Hans von Bülow, which was planned for the following spring, Richter was engaged as chorus master. For this *première* Wagner left his voluntary exile in Triebschen for the first time to come to Munich, and it was to be the greatest triumph of his life. He wrote about it to his faithful housekeeper Vreneli:

Yesterday's performance was a glorious feast such as I shall probably never experience again. From the beginning to the end I had to be present at the side of the King in the Royal Box, from where I also had to acknowledge the ovations of the public. Nothing like it has ever happened before or anywhere.

As this was breach of all rules as laid down by court ceremonial, it naturally received many malicious comments from the hostile press.

Eight years were to pass before Wagner saw his King again. When finally Hans von Bülow filed the suit for divorce against his wife and resigned from his Munich position at the same time, the situation was clarified. Ludwig was deeply hurt. For the rest of his life the fascination of Wagner's magic world kept him spellbound, and he continued to give assistance to the artist who had created this world in every way; but in future he avoided the man Wagner who had deceived him. A purely emotional factor may also have played its part, namely plain jealousy which could be explained by the King's notorious homosexual tendencies. From now on he sought to gratify his romantically artistic dreams in other fields, and he devoted his interest in the main to those fantastic mediaeval castles which he built in the Bavarian Alps and which brought him to the brink of ruin. Except in transit and on brief business visits Wagner never came to Munich again.

Now that *Die Meistersinger* had been completed and performed, Wagner turned to the most monumental work of his life, the completion of the *Ring des Nibelungen*. It is a miracle that he was capable of continuing *Siegfried* after an interruption of twelve years without any noticeable feel of a stylistic break. The domestic idyll in Triebschen was his world, and he did not allow any disturbance from outside to impinge on it. Another daughter, Eva, had been born in 1867, and lastly his son Siegfried in 1869. One year later, after Cosima's divorce had become absolute, she was married to Wagner.

It is always of interest to compare different views on the same subject. This is what Glasenapp, the accredited biographer of Wahnfried, has to say about this event:

No union should be more sacred to every German, neither has any such union ever been concluded with greater unselfishness, with more lofty, supra-personal aims—nor after such hard struggles. This great exile had been driven from place to place by the stupidity and unkindness of the world around him, who even envied him the favours of his King and sent him into a new banishment. Now, before God and the world, he was united with that noble woman who knew no petty and undignified human fear, but who had entered into his life as the saving, celestial power of love.

By contrast one single comment: an extract from a letter (originally in French) which von Bülow wrote to Comtesse Charnacé, Cosima's sister, on 15 September 1869:

Believe me, I have done everything humanly possible to avoid a public scandal. For more than three years I have lived a life of indescribable torment. You simply cannot imagine the consuming agitations to which I was continuously subjected. In the end I sacrificed my whole artistic and material existence. The only thing left to sacrifice was my life—that, I must confess, would have been the simplest method of solving the problem, of cutting this complex knot. This sacrifice I was not prepared to make—can anyone blame me? But perhaps I would even have taken this course of action if, on the part of that other one who is as sublime in his works as he is unspeakably low in his deeds, I had discovered the least trace of honour, just one expression of some basic feeling of decency. . . . When in November I addressed an almost indiscreet question to Cosima about her sudden departure, she considered it fair to reply to me with a lie. It was only a few months ago that, through the press, I came to know of the Master's good fortune that his mistress (whose name was given in full) had at long last presented him with a son who was to be christened Siegfried as a good omen for the completion of his new opera. I have thus been crowned most magnificently with the horns of a cuckold. Unfortunately I could not flee from Munich—but the tortures of hell which I have had to suffer there during the last months of my activity cannot be imagined. . . . I only had the choice of two alternatives: either be treated with degrading pity as an

D

individual who had no idea of things which were common knowledge, or else be considered so infamous as to be the protégé of the royal protégé at such a price. . . .

The reader may draw his own conclusions.

Whilst in his seclusion at Triebschen Wagner was working on *Siegfried*, Munich was preparing *Das Rheingold*, which was to be succeeded by *Die Walküre* six months later. This plan had been agreed on between him and the King, but it was upset by von Bülow's divorce and resignation. Wagner would have no further truck either with Munich, the headquarters of the whole derogatory campaign against him, Cosima and von Bülow, or with the royal *Hoftheater* where the management was not obsequious enough to him and his demands for unrestricted authority. His old pet dream for Munich—the building of a theatre especially adapted to his purposes, for which his Zürich friend Gottfried Semper had already made a model—had vanished together with Hans von Bülow. Originally Wagner had no objections on principle to separate performances of the individual works which constitute the *Ring*, and after von Bülow had left he entrusted his amanuensis Hans Richter with the direction of *Rheingold*. But events took a different turn. It is difficult to free oneself of the impression that Wagner had decided to sabotage the performance and that he used the young, inexperienced Hans Richter, so unquestioningly devoted to his Master, as an unwitting tool. Wagner protested by telegram that the stage machinery was inadequate and unreliable, and the performance was cancelled after the dress rehearsal. Hans Richter had refused to accept any instructions whatsoever from the management, as he claimed that he was solely responsible to the Master, and the King sacked him without notice. As Ludwig was not prepared under any circumstances to forgo the performance, it took place several weeks later on 22 September 1869. Franz Wüllner conducted—the repetiteur at the *Hoftheater* and the only man who dared oppose Wagner's wishes. A few weeks before the outbreak of the Franco-Prussian war, on 26 June 1870, *Die Walküre* followed, again under the baton of Franz Wüllner who was quite unconcerned about Wagner's interdict and excommunication. The King had won.

Wagner countered with—Bayreuth!

To Louis Schindelmeisser, a friend of his youth, he had once written:

> I do not want to offer pleasant entertainment; I want to spread terror and emotion, for in no other way can I affect the humanity of our day. . . . Whoever deals with me must be able and prepared to play *va banque*, to stake his all on one card . . . because my works are the products of a person who is interested in only one gamble: either break the bank, or ruin yourself utterly. I do not wish for a "comfortable life" with great renown and a good income.

At least one cannot say of him that he took his risks without eyes wide open. As so often before, he had risked everything and had lost. His stubborn opposition to the Munich performances had been of no avail. Repeatedly he had asked Ludwig for a personal audience, but the King had avoided such a meeting: from experience he was afraid of what Minna had termed the "admirable blarney" of her husband, and he did not feel himself strong enough to resist Wagner's voluble persuasion and his dominant personality. The Master was visibly annoyed and made no secret of it to the King. He refused to deliver the *Siegfried* score, although according to an agreement of 1864 he was contractually obliged to do so, as the King, in return for the subsidies paid by the treasury, was entitled to the possession of all Wagner's future works. Wagner's excuse that the music still had to be polished up could not be refuted, and if the worst came to the worst, he was always ready with the threat that he would retire completely into solitude and poverty—a threat which with his generous patron never failed to have the desired effect.

Meanwhile, as the last part of his tetralogy—*Götterdämmerung* —was slowly beginning to mature, Wagner's other plans were also showing signs of coming to fruition. His design was not only a blow at Munich, but above all a foundation which would free him once and for all from this detested dependence and at the same time make him king of his own empire. The choice of locality was due to pure chance: in a volume of the Brockhaus encyclopaedia he had found mention of a rococo theatre in Bayreuth, once the residence of a Markgraf. In April 1871 he visited this friendly little town with Cosima. The opera house proved to be of no use whatsoever for his contemporary purposes, but local conditions appeared to him to be favourable, so Wagner made a quick decision and took the necessary preliminary steps to start an enterprise the audacity of which left nothing to be desired. A society of supporters was to get together the necessary means to build a theatre and put on festivals along the lines of his Zürich dreams. The Bayreuth Mayor, Muncker, and the financier Feustel were enthusiastic about the project, and they decided to invite the patronage of 1000 subscribers: anyone who guaranteed a sum of 300 *Taler* would have free admission to the first festival, which was to take place in summer 1873.

The foundation stone of the festival theatre, the *Festspieltheater*, was laid on 22 May 1872. The occasion was celebrated by a performance of Beethoven's Ninth under Wagner's own direction, and building began immediately afterwards.

Seen from a financial point of view, this venture had precisely the same negative result as the rest of Wagner's undertakings. Throughout the then German *Reich* Wagner Societies were founded to raise funds for the Bayreuth idea, and there was no lack of Wagnerians; but the "patronage subscriptions" found no market. The building, which had been started on promissory notes, got stuck in its initial stages. Since the victorious progress of *Die Meistersinger* Wagner's stature had assumed super-human dimensions. Untiringly, in word and music, he wooed supporters for his great plans, conducted concerts for his Bayreuth fund and coerced all his friends to assist him. But in the last resort there was no way out but to appeal to King Ludwig, and finally the King undertook to cover the entire deficit, thereby making it possible for the building of the *Festspieltheater* to continue.

Amidst all this worry and excitement Wagner completed the score of *Götterdämmerung* on 21 November 1874. The necessary rehearsals were agreed with the personnel, which had been recruited from all over the country, for the following summer, and the first Festival was fixed for August 1876. Together with the theatre Wagner had a house of his own built in Bayreuth, Villa Wahnfried, into which he could move in April 1874. He was his own lord and master, responsible to no-one, and now at a height which hardly any other artist had ever achieved before him. But this last and greatest victory had cost a tremendous effort. The years of strife and care, the Herculean labours which still lay ahead of him in the preparation of the Festival and the endless, exhausting battles he had to fight afterwards—for the Festival resulted in a considerable financial loss—all this undermined his health and probably shortened his life by years.

The great event of the first Bayreuth Festival (13–30 August 1876) is a milestone in the history of opera. Of the visitors to the Festival the highest dignitary was Wilhelm I, the German Emperor. Wagner met him on his arrival in Bayreuth, and the words which Wilhelm addressed to Wagner may well have coincided with everyone's thoughts: "I never believed that you would make it." On this occasion Wagner saw King Ludwig again for the first time since the memorable *Meistersinger* performance in Munich. The King had already attended the dress rehearsals, and during the first of these—for *Rheingold*— Wagner made a concession to his royal patron: he excluded all other listeners. By now Ludwig had become an eccentric, and it was his habit to command performances just for himself in an otherwise empty theatre, as he could not stand exposing himself as the focal point of staring curiosity. After all that had happened, his personal attitude towards Wagner was aloof, although he retained his old enthusiasm for the music.

Once more Wagner had to lay claim on Ludwig's generosity. As has been mentioned, the Festival ended with a considerable deficit, and Wagner's next care was to cover this loss, but without success. As a magnanimous gesture von Bülow donated 40,000 *Mark*, the proceeds of a concert tour, to the Bayreuth fund, but this as well as the sums Wagner could raise himself by concerts was a trifle in comparison with the deficit of 150,000 *Mark* which had to be covered—not to speak of the further capital which had to be found before the next Festival could be envisaged. An attempt to win the support of the government of the *Reich* came to nought, and six years had to go by before the *Festspielhaus* opened its doors again.

From all these worries Wagner escaped by taking refuge in a new creation which demanded every ounce of his energy. It was his last work, *Parsifal*, the first conception of which also goes back to that inexhaustibly creative Dresden period. By spring 1879 the music was sketched out and the score was finished by the beginning of 1882. The Bayreuth problems were finally again resolved by King Ludwig; he took responsibility for the burden of the remaining deficit and also put the choir and orchestra of his *Hoftheater* at the disposal of the new Festival, which was to take place in summer 1882. The enterprise was saved, and the King also had the generosity to fulfil Wagner's insistent request: he waived his right to have *Parsifal* repeated in Munich, as it was of greatest importance to Wagner that this work, because of its particular character, should be reserved for Bayreuth alone. On 12 November 1881 he performed the Prelude to *Parsifal* with the Munich orchestra for his royal friend, and this was their last meeting. Wagner was no courtier, which is quite pardonable, but on this occasion he hurt his benefactor quite unnecessarily. When asked to repeat the *Parsifal* Prelude, as the King wished to hear it a second time, Wagner gave in with obvious ill grace; but when Ludwig also asked to hear the *Lohengrin* Prelude which he loved particularly, the Master handed the baton to *Hofkapellmeister* Levi (who happened to be present) and left the rostrum. It gave him pleasure to perform his latest composition to the King, but he had no mind to accept orders from him.

Wagner had the illusion that with the issue of his "Bayreuth Patronage Subscriptions" he would be able to hold at bay the ordinary opera public which he loathed and only play his works to friends and enthusiasts of his art. As the subscription scheme had foundered, there was nothing else to be done but throw open the second Bayreuth Festival—during which *Parsifal* was to be performed sixteen times—to the public at large by the sale of tickets. His dilemma was insoluble: he considered the ordinary opera theatres damnable institutions, yet he was dependent on them. His earlier operas up to *Lohengrin* he had to surrender to these theatres, which to him was a disgraceful humiliation. Since the material aspects of his life had become

assured, he made many difficulties, but still he allowed his works
to be played elsewhere because his need of money was boundless.
He once wrote to Heinrich Laube:

> I have the lowest opinion of the efficacy of the existing
> German theatres and hold the decided view that these
> theatres, no matter how they may be directed, can only
> increase the confusion and corruption of German artistic
> taste. I am resolved not to have anything further to do with
> them—except in the event of some work of mine being staged,
> when I shall do everything in my power, in order to get a
> good performance, to have to deal with a less uncouth and
> somewhat more helpful person than the one whom I now
> find in charge of the theatre in Munich.

And another time: "Under no circumstances will I ever again
write a work for one of our opera theatres or leave it to them for
performance. With *Die Meistersinger* I have had my last contact
with those theatres."

Needless to add that he broke his word: one cannot keep a
nonsensical promise. On top of it, and despite all royal favours,
his insatiable need of money was greater than the bee in his
bonnet. After the first Bayreuth Festival he not only allowed the
Ring to be staged in any theatre which was prepared to produce
the whole cycle, but he even made concessions regarding
individual performances. More than that, he allowed himself
to be persuaded to grant an enterprising man of the theatre—
Angelo Neumann, director of the Leipzig Opera—the right to
form a touring ensemble and perform the *Ring* throughout
Germany, and later the whole of Europe. This venture proved
highly lucrative.

The Festival of 1882 was no less magnificent than the first
one and even ended with a surplus, due to the much smaller
stage requirements. A repetition of the Festival in the following
year was assured. But Wagner's state of health was seriously
shaken—and for several years he had suffered increasingly from
a heart complaint. During the last performance of *Parsifal* the
conductor Hermann Levi was taken ill. Wagner himself took

the baton for the third act—in the covered orchestra pit he was
unnoticed by the public—and conducted the work to the end.
In a way this was his true Farewell to Life.

He was very deeply hurt that this Festival was not graced by
King Ludwig's presence, but Ludwig was ailing, and his
aversion to public appearances was almost insuperable.
Presumably he also remembered well the affront which Wagner
had offered him in Munich. Relations between the King and
his family had been strained for a long time, and at times he
was the despair of his ministers, for he tried to avoid the burdens
of state as far as he possibly could. His tragic fate is well known:
on medical evidence he was declared certifiable in 1886 and
kept under strict surveillance. Nowadays there are doubts
whether he was really insane: of the four doctors on the
strength of whose diagnosis he had been declared a paranoiac,
not one had as much as seen him, and their verdict was merely
based on the statements of servants and courtiers. Only
a few days later he found his death in Lake Starnberg while
boating with the hated doctor who was supervising him, and
whom he pulled into the water with him. It is impossible to
differentiate between an act of desperation and an act of
insanity.

By that time Wagner was no longer amongst the living. After
the *Parsifal* Festival he was in urgent need of rest and spent the
winter in Venice where, with his family, he lived in the sumptu-
ous Palazzo Vendramin. His energies were unimpaired and he
worked on several essays. This last winter brought forth a
report about *Das Bühnenweihfestspiel in Bayreuth* ("The Consecra-
tion Drama in Bayreuth"), a fragment *Über das Weibliche im
Menschen* ("The Feminine in Man"), and a contribution for a
weekly *Über die Wiederaufführung eines Jugendwerks* ("About the
Performance of an Early Work"). It was the symphony which
he had composed and performed at the age of nineteen in
Leipzig. For long the score had been considered lost, but it
turned up again by pure chance. With the pupils of the Liceo
Benedetto Marcello he played the work on Christmas Day,
Cosima's birthday, to his family and a few invited friends,
amongst them Liszt who had come on a visit. His interest in
everything which came within his ken was undiminished, and

so was his physical condition when he had a good day. But the sands had run out. He suffered from cramps for which his doctor knew no cure; they occurred with increasing frequency and caused great concern. On 13 February 1883 a heart attack put an end to his life.

PART II

THE MAN AND HIS MUSIC

DUALITY OF CHARACTER

THE WHOLE COURSE of Wagner's life was of a fantastic individuality, characterized by the fusion within one person of two utterly disparate and unusual talents raised to their highest potential: the tremendous impetus and the invincible, outwardly-directed energy of the great statesman, politician or reformer, coupled with the ability of the immortal artist to concentrate completely and solely, with utter devotion and total lack of concern for all external circumstances, on the work he is creating. He was two personalities rolled into one: when it came to imposing his will on the world he was Caesar, Mahomet, Napoleon, Bismarck—when it came to the work which had taken hold of his imagination to the exclusion of everything else he was Michelangelo, Goethe, Beethoven. Different periods of his life served one or other of these purposes. It is obvious that the "artistic politician" to a certain extent paved the way for the artist, for no unworldly dreamer could ever have won victories as he did. On the other hand the artist had to suffer again and again under the understandable enmities which are the everyday lot of the politician. It is impossible to battle against the world without provoking the bitterest of reactions.

These two manifestations of Wagner's nature may appear to be incompatible, but they had a common root: an incredibly strong, instinctive desire to dominate. Paradoxical though it may sound, the splendid ethos of the artist and the utter lack of scruples of the man were emanations of one and the same original urge. On the one hand they led to artistic perfection, to the achievement of the highest attainments of which his talent was capable—and on the other to this uninhibited exploitation of every imaginable advantage in the fight for his bare existence. A lot of nonsense is talked by those who want to separate the man from the artist. They are both one single individual, for they think, they feel, they act as an entity. But in the special case of Wagner—which may well be unique—the manifestations of the man and the artist were extreme contrasts, even though they issued from the same source. Wagner was Narcissus. Every one of his utterances, his whole demeanour, the graceful élan of his handwriting reflect it, and they had to be subservient to his work and his very thought. Every letter which he wrote was written with care and with an unmistakeable sense of making an impression, and in the same way he would spend any amount of time and energy on the clean copy of a score. For his later works—*Siegfried*, *Götterdämmerung*, *Parsifal*— he first made a pencil sketch, then a sketch of the score, and in the end wrote out a full score, and each of these clean copies is a masterpiece of artistically individual calligraphy. His self-love was sublimated in his love for his work, for every bar and every word which formed part of it. Just as for his own person only the best and the most expensive would serve so he also applied the precision of a goldsmith, of a Benvenuto Cellini, to every detail of his scores. Like his thoughts, his writing—the concrete expression of his thoughts—was guided by a determined feeling for form and beauty. At the end of the *Meistersinger* score he put down "Triebschen, Thursday, 24 October 1867, in the evening at 8 o'clock", and did so in the knowledge that this was an event of cosmic consequence. Similarly, on the compositional sketch of *Götterdämmerung* of which he made a present to King Ludwig, he wrote a *Rheingold* quotation: *Vollendet das ewige Werk!* ("Completed, the eternal work!") Everything concerning him and his work was of incomparable importance. All this has made his work great—and not only the work, but also the man, as was inevitable in the case of one so obsessed with himself.

There is no human being who does not want to show off somehow or other, but in general this basic requisite for self-preservation is compensated for in the parallelogram of spiritual forces and is thereby under control. When this urge to show off becomes as disproportionate as in the case of Wagner, it can become a public nuisance and even a danger. It was only his artistic genius which prevented the worst, because it opened a safety valve as an outlet for the colossal pressure of those forces. As a rule every outstanding spiritual talent finds its own specific area of activity which, in the case of most great men of mind and culture, becomes productive and neutralizes this urge for power; only an insignificant portion of their energy remains for the battle of existence. In the field of music Bach, Haydn, Mozart, Beethoven, Schubert are obvious examples. Of course, external circumstances are not irrelevant, and the theatre has always been an arena of battles and intrigues. Opera composers such as Händel, Gluck and Verdi have been compelled just as early as Wagner to learn how to defend their own skin.

But with Wagner, pugnacity was part of his nature. Even in his earliest beginnings his fight for recognition ran parallel with his creative efforts, and at times he devoted his very best energies to precisely this fight. Perhaps it was only the fact that his sources of inspiration dried up occasionally which turned him into a theoretician and propaganda writer, but initially the two went hand in hand. The young Wagner was his own indefatigable propagandist. He always knew how to handle a pen and could make his point with apparently uncontradictable logic. He certainly wrote the longest musician's letters in existence. A prime example of Wagner's persuasive verbosity is a letter which, at the age of twenty, he wrote to Franz Hauser, producer at the Leipzig theatre: in print it takes up eight pages and had no success whatsoever. In it he defended his early opera *Die Feen* which Hauser had turned down. A couple of years later, from Magdeburg, he sent a report to Robert Schumann, who was then editor of the highly respected Leipzig *Neue Zeitschrift für Musik*. The main theme of this epistle was his own opera *Das Liebesverbot*, which he himself had staged and performed, and he wrote:

> With the best will in the world I could not avoid saying a few things about myself. After all, considering that I am the musical director here, I had to mention myself in a musical report about Magdeburg, and also it would be ridiculous to run myself down without having deserved it. But the third and special reason why I write about my opera is that

otherwise no one else will do so—and I would like a few words to be said about it.

And cautiously he added: "Nevertheless I am sure you will agree that my name [as author] must on no account be mentioned, otherwise woe betide me." In later years he often made use of anonymity, and it is invariably a sign that his conscience pricked him. In his early stages all his endeavours were directed towards one single ambition: to be a success. About *Das Liebesverbot* he went and wrote to his Leipzig friend Theodor Apel:

> This opera must be a resounding success, so that I can gain both fame and money. Once I have achieved this aim, armed with both, you and I will go to Italy in the spring of 1836. In Italy I shall compose an Italian opera or even more, depending on how things turn out, and once we are strong and sun-tanned we shall make our way to France. In Paris I shall compose a French opera, and the Lord only knows how far I will have got by then!

Quite clearly his imagination was miles ahead of him. On the basis of similar suppositions he also tackled *Rienzi* in Riga, because a work of such dimensions and technical demands could only be performed with the resources of the Paris *Opéra*. Therefore, according to his calculations— and this is where his optimism made him blind to logical reasoning—Paris cannot possibly hesitate to stage a work which makes such demands.

One thing he obviously learnt early on: the secret of rhetoric. He was inordinately proud of this talent. As a rule, his will-power was stronger than that of his opponent and so, as often as not, he had his way. It is no mean achievement to get an instrument out of a piano manufacturer by sheer gift of the gab —but he did it, as he told Mathilde Wesendonck in a letter:

> There is something very special about this instrument. You know how long I have wanted it, but in vain. Nor is it strange that when I went to Paris last year... I suddenly had the idea to try for such a piano with all my energy. No other

purpose was as serious to me, everything else of secondary importance, no other plan did I follow up with such eagerness. My visit to Madame Erard was quite different. I was thoroughly inspired when talking to these simple, unimportant people and, as I heard later, I completely won them over by my own enthusiasm. I became the possessor of the instrument almost in passing, as though it were a joke. Oh, wonderful instinct of nature! It really always manifests itself as the instinct of self-preservation and adapts itself to each individual, each character.

His own instinct of self-preservation always manifested itself as a continual spur towards success, and his mania to be successful with women is only a very natural outcome of this urge. With extraordinary naïveté he reports in his memoirs a youthful episode which has nothing to commend it except the clarity of his powers of self-assessment. When he was twenty and at the theatre in Würzburg, he made the acquaintance of the fiancée of one of the orchestral musicians during the course of a dance. He courted her . . .

. . . until it came to pass that, in the general excitement we, too, felt free of all personal considerations, and we found ourselves embracing and kissing while the official lover was playing for the dance. Her fiancé noticed the uninhibited tenderness which Friederike bestowed on me, and the fact that he accepted his lot with sadness but without actual opposition for the first time released within me a flattering feeling of self-esteem. Never before had I found any reason to allow myself the conceited assumption that I might make a favourable impression on a young girl. In my association with my male contemporaries I had, in the course of time, gained a certain self-confidence: my considerable vitality and my constant excitability had at last made me conscious, in my contacts with all those whom I met, of a certain feeling of power, and that I was capable either of inflaming the enthusiasm of my more sluggish companions, or else of stunning them. It was from the silently suffering reticence of this poor oboist, when he became aware of the ardent

overtures which his betrothed made to me, that I gained—
as I said—the first impression that I might have some
attraction not only for men, but also for women.

Wagner was of small stature and not particularly prepossessing.
It was his imposing profile, the spirituality of his features with
which in later life he made such an impression. When still
young, the knowledge that he was not outwardly good-looking
must have awakened a desire to call attention to himself. In the
report quoted above the most significant fact is that, more than
thirty years later and therefore after a lapse of time which ought
to make an objective verdict possible, Wagner did not evidence
the faintest trace of remorse for having hurt the fiancé who was
his friend and the victim of this flirtation. On the contrary, this
circumstance formed part of his smug satisfaction, and it must
be stated quite plainly that this innocent occurrence serves as a
perfect model for the attitude which remained characteristic for
Wagner in the later and more serious love-affairs of his life—
be it with Jessie Laussot, Mathilde Wesendonck, Cosima von
Bülow. Incidentally, the poor husbands whom Wagner had
cuckolded never cut a very dashing figure in his memoirs. This
even applies to generous Otto Wesendonck who, at the time,
straightened out matters after the event with the greatest
delicacy and tact, and for whom Wagner had nothing but
derogatory and disparaging remarks.

There is a not unnatural tendency in many cases to condemn
Wagner's conduct on moral grounds, and it is necessary to say
something on this subject as a matter of principle. Moral
concepts are of no earthly use when considering the phenomenon
of a man who has no inkling of such concepts. His feelings were
of such impulsive intensity, his whole way of thinking so utterly
egocentric, that there was no room at all for any other feelings,
any other thoughts than those which concerned himself. His
lack of moral inhibitions was near-grandiose, and it must
be acknowledged that the unbridled impetuosity which it
unleashed also gave that immense intensity to his musical
utterance which is the secret of its effect.

There are animal lovers who condemn the fox for raiding the
chicken-run and the cat for killing birds. It would be equally

naïve to rebuke Wagner for actions which normally would be considered the acts of a scoundrel. He had the innocence of a wild animal.

There can scarcely be any doubt that the years of destitution in Paris had affected his inner being very decisively. His ego had been mortally wounded during that period, for he was utterly convinced of his abilities and capabilities, and yet he had been treated like a troublesome beggar to whom at best one gives a little something as a sop. He never succeeded in forgiving Paris that treatment meted out to him, and yet that town always continued to have a magic attraction for him. His hatred against Paris and—as he called it—the French "bastard nature" found its individual target in the person of Meyerbeer whom he identified with that nature. At one time he had admired him, and not only from motivations of policy: *Rienzi* is an undeniable testimonial of this admiration, and traces of it can still be found in *Der fliegende Holländer*. But a mere two years later he was very touchy on that subject and did not like it at all when the matter was commented upon—especially if the comment happened to come from Schumann, whose critical rejection of Meyerbeer he well knew. With regard to a criticism of *Der fliegende Holländer* he wrote to him:

Incidentally, I agree with everything you say about my opera as far as you know the work to date. Only one thing has frightened me and—I admit it freely—embittered me, because of the root of the matter: that you calmly tell me much of it had the flavour of—Meyerbeer. I simply do not know what on earth is supposed to be "Meyerbeerian", unless it be a crafty endeavour to achieve a shallow popularity. . . . The fact that you say this is a clear indication that your attitude towards me is in no way unprejudiced. Perhaps this is due to your knowledge of the external circumstances of my life, as these have in fact brought me into a personal relationship with the man Meyerbeer, and I owe him a certain gratitude.

With increasing years Wagner's German nationalism became more and more pronounced, and without any doubt the Paris experiences are at the root of it. Twenty years later the *Tannhäuser* scandal in Paris furnished further fuel to those emotions. His feelings towards the French people and their character were very closely intertwined with a personal desire of revenge—this is evinced by the most pitiable literary product of which he was ever guilty: a supposedly humorous dramatic parody, entitled *Eine Kapitulation*, in which in 1871 he derided the French defeat. He actually tried (anonymously, of course) to have this piece of bad taste performed in Berlin, but fortunately no theatre was prepared to stage it, and it is incomprehensible that several years later he incorporated it in the publication of his Collected Works. A case such as this shows up with special clarity the unbridled intensity of his emotional life; sheer hatred befuddles his senses to the point where he is incapable of taking an objective, rational view of his own actions. Incidentally, his francophobia found a representative in yet another composer: Offenbach. In general Wagner had a good judgment of music which breathed genuine originality and invention, despite the understandable one-sidedness in a man of his character, and in this respect he was decidedly fair, for example, towards Rossini and even Auber; but Offenbach made his hackles rise. As a personal favour to young Weissheimer who was conducting the performance, he attended Offenbach's "Orpheus in the Underworld" in Mainz and wrote about it: "I was truly horrified that my interest in this young man should have brought me down to the level of witnessing such a piece of ghastliness, and for a long time I could not help showing Weissheimer my displeasure in a most obvious manner." And Glasenapp, with understanding concurrence, reports Wagner as saying during the last year of his life, regarding the then sensational catastrophe when the *Ringtheater* in Vienna caught fire and 900 people lost their lives during a performance of Offenbach's "Tales of Hoffmann":

All the people sitting together in such a theatre are mere good-for-nothings. When miners in a coal pit are buried alive, I am deeply moved and horrified, and I am filled with disgust for a society which obtains its means of heating in such a manner. But it leaves me cold, and hardly moves me, when a certain number of that crowd perish while listening to an Offenbach operetta which does not offer one iota of moral worth.

His attitude towards Offenbach, in parenthesis, is another facet of Wagner's lack of sensibility which is symptomatic for his time and age, the age in which romanticism was at its height and when people had a stereotyped attitude towards drama which one is tempted to describe as a "mania for the gruesome". It would appear that at that time the theatre-going public was not satisfied unless there were quite a few fatalities. In his youthful drama *Leubold und Adelaide* Wagner had exterminated entire families, and in the last act some of the victims had to make their re-appearance as ghosts in order to keep the action going. Admittedly, this was infantile, but it was a sign of the times and the fashion prevailed for a surprisingly long time. Even in the early years of this century it was still possible, on All Souls' Day, to go to a suburban Viennese theatre to a performance of Raupach's *Der Müller und sein Kind* for a liberal dose of goose pimples. It seems that Wagner had no sense whatsoever for the fact that even in drama a *détente* is possible. He called *Siegfried* a "comedy"—after all, there are only two casualties, Fafner and Mime in Act II, and they are no great loss. In *Tristan* finally only King Marke and Brangäne are left alive to bewail the dead, and when it comes to the end of *Götterdämmerung* (forgetting for the moment about poor unfortunate Gutrune) of all the Gods and humans, giants and dwarfs who are the motivating force of that great tetralogy which is the *Ring*, we are left only with Alberich and the three Rhine Maidens, whose hanky-panky started the whole trouble in the first scene of *Rheingold*. No dramatist has ever polished off all his heroes in more summary a fashion.

In his memoirs Wagner touched on an episode from his Zürich days which is utterly typical in this context:

Once again, during these winter evenings, I read *Tristan* to another circle of friends. Gottfried Keller was particularly pleased by the taut form of the whole, for actually there are only three fully developed scenes. But Semper [the architect who later built the *Festspielhaus* in Bayreuth] got annoyed about it: he accused me of taking everything too seriously, and said that the finest element of the artistic organization of such a theme consisted in interrupting its intense seriousness, so that despite his deeply emotional involvement the listener could find pleasure. This was what he liked so much in Mozart's *Don Giovanni*, that there the tragic types appeared as though at a masquerade; he said that he even preferred the domino to a character mask. I admitted that I could make things much easier for myself if I were to take life more seriously, art however somewhat more lightly, but also that by now I would probably choose to stick to the inverse concept.

Semper could not know that the original, from which Wagner borrowed his *Tristan* story (the great epic by Gottfried von Strassburg) actually contains many gay and even burlesque episodes, but it gives food for thought that, in his unassumedness and his lack of specialized knowledge in matters of that particular form of art, he was able to give the musical dramatist a lesson regarding Mozart's greatness.

Paris had taught Wagner a lesson the hard way, and it had remained engraved on his mind: it was not merely important to create a work, but even more to get it properly performed. In Dresden he had gained the authority which stamps the mark of leadership on an artist. In this regard he was assisted as much by his innate talent as a conductor as by the success of his works. For many years his satisfaction about both had kept him reconciled to his activities and had therefore furthered the intense productivity of this period during which the creative artist, proceeding from *Tannhäuser* to *Lohengrin*, could mould that style which now became utterly personal, and at the same time could collect a wealth of material, of fertile inspirations, which were to last him for the rest of his life. Apart from those subjects on which he based his later, complete works, he also conceived a *Wieland der Schmied*, a *Jesus von Nazareth* at that time, and in addition a Buddhist subject, *Die Sieger*, which still occupied his mind during his Munich days. And so this energetic, organizing, scheming, indefatigably argumentative person grew into a personality whom some followed un-

questioningly, but whom most mistrusted. In addition it became
evident that such a restless, limitlessly ambitious character,
intolerant when it came to any restriction whatsoever, could not
become a mere cog in the wheels of an organization of any kind.
The rebellious Saxon subject would have become an equally
rebellious Republican, and he himself saw the truth of this
matter very soon.

The Dresden revolution had uprooted Wagner, but not only
as far as the ordinary course of his everyday life was concerned.
As has been mentioned earlier, it took him five years before the
musician within himself could regain his creative urge. Those
five years were the main period of his "politico-artistic"
activities; they were dedicated to theoretical writings, but his
actual aim was the promotion of his work, his ideas, his future
plans, and to gather a band of friends and adherents. Like
every such party, his own also began with only a handful of
followers, but within a few years it developed into a powerful
factor in German musical life. Originally the soul of this party
was Liszt who assembled a group of young enthusiasts around
him in Weimar and tirelessly—in word, writing and deed—
spread the gospel of the *Zukunftsmusik*. This term "Music of the
Future" had been borrowed by a spiteful critic from Wagner's
book *Das Kunstwerk der Zukunft*, and Liszt adopted it with pride.
The battle for and against the *Zukunftsmusik* has by now become
a matter of music history. As its most essential principle it
stressed the poetically expressive elements in music as opposed
to abstract form, and in this connection it tended towards descriptive, extra-musical influences in the formative process.
Tendencies of this nature, which found their first and greatest
protagonists in Liszt and Berlioz, could not but represent the
most welcome fulfilment to Wagner with his imaginative originality and his highly developed intensity of expression. Without
any doubt Wagner was not only the most significant musician of
that group, but with his theoretical writings he also provided it
with a clear-cut programme and a philosophical, aesthetic justification. Liszt was sufficiently magnanimous to acknowledge
Wagner's superiority with enthusiastic admiration, and he
never wearied in his efforts for his exiled friend (for whom also,
incidentally, he made more than one substantial material

sacrifice) from the time of Wagner's flight from Dresden until that unhappy occurrence during Wagner's stay in Venice of which mention has already been made (cf. p. 64). Wagner on his part, even during his absence, took good care that the "party" was always kept informed, and on occasion he gave instructions to the editor Brendel of the *Neue Zeitschrift für Musik* in Leipzig, who had taken over the editorship from Schumann and had become a sort of journalistic publicist of the "Musicians of the Future". A letter from Wagner to his friend Uhlig in Dresden, who also worked for the *Neue Zeitschrift*, reads like a directive from a party leader to the organiser of his party:

> In future, my dear friend, the *Zeitung für Musik* must report only along those lines: you can see how much there is to be said. The main thing is always to adhere to the principle which I stated in my letters to Brendel: "All music should be exalted, supported and promoted if it develops in a direction towards poetry, but whenever it deviates from that direction such erroneous and mistaken trends should be proven and condemned."

Now is perhaps the moment to give some details, if only in brief, about Wagner's theoretical ideas. His writings are heavy going for any reader, not only because of the long-winded verbosity with which he expounds his historical, philosophical, aesthetic arguments, but above all because, whenever he starts theorizing, his otherwise clear and plastic style becomes incredibly pompous and involved. The reader must be convinced at all cost; so he bombards him with arguments, and the more dubious his basic supposition, the more he has to engage in rhetoric in order to achieve the desired result. Whenever Wagner gets effusive there is every justification to mistrust his reasoning.

Again and again he comes back to one—to him!—fundamental fact: the utter bankruptcy of modern art. To August Röckel, his fellow-revolutionary of Dresden days who corresponded with Wagner from prison, he wrote: "Only now is it becoming evident how infamous and, frankly, worthless the whole of our present-day 'art' truly is, now that it has discarded the last vestige of modesty . . . ." He regarded Greek drama as the ideal form because, as the perfect expression of a national soul, it could unite the entire nation in true religious and artistic devotion. In its modern development art had become a commercialized affair, the theatre nothing but an entertainment. Only by re-unifying all forms of art in the *Gesamtkunstwerk*, the "Work of Art of the Future", would humanity be able to regain salvation and true culture. As a result of recent developments the theatre had become "literary drama" by adopting one direction, opera by adopting another. Both were contemptible: the former because it lacked that soul which can only be supplied by music as the indispensable emotional element, the latter because it was a travesty of dramatic art, its most despicable and degenerate manifestation. The root of the evil lay in the fact that drama, the ultimate end of the art of the stage, had been made the means, whereas the means—music—had been turned into an end of its own. Even the greatest products of this hybrid species, the works of Gluck, Mozart, Beethoven, Weber, could have no bearing on this fundamental concept: the original concept was wrong, and in addition—Wagner stressed this particular detail repeatedly—opera was a Franco-Italian mongrel, completely un-German and an imported article, reprehensible both morally and artistically, the fostering of which brought disgrace to the German nation. According to Wagner, Mozart in his *Zauberflöte*, Beethoven in *Fidelio*, Weber in *Freischütz* and *Euryanthe* made magnificent attempts to create a German opera, but they could not succeed because they lacked a prerequisite: a real dramatic line without any concessions, and a truly German style of declamation and representation.

These, reduced to their barest bones, are Wagner's basic principles. They have their positive and their negative aspect: on the one hand there is the vision of the goal, though still vague, of the true music drama of Wagner's imagination; on the other the polemics against everything which had been achieved thus far and must be overcome. In a letter to the Weimar *Intendant* von Zigesar he gave his own commentary:

In order to present this ideal in its most clearly discernible purity, I must completely unshackle it from every influence of what has gone before. I must therefore first negate all that which already exists and expose its futility, in order to gain the ground on which my ideal can take root and be comprehended in such a way that out of sheer conviction I can gain the strength and the courage to take the next step towards achieving my ideal, i.e. to create something new.

By far the largest part of the discussion is concerned with proving that the prevailing form of art has to be overcome, and he arrives at the most amazing conclusions, all of which have to serve as proof that the whole development up to the present has been along the wrong lines. In his *Faust* Goethe had needed music in order to give expression to that which was inexpressible in mere words; consequently all drama after Goethe was superfluous. In his last symphony, his Ninth, Beethoven had to have recourse to the human voice because he had reached the limit of what could be said by instruments alone; therefore any symphony after Beethoven is erroneous, useless, superfluous. Painting and sculpture, like all minor and more intimate manifestations of music, are a matter of idle bourgeois entertainment, and fostering them can only result in a waste and dissipation of those forces which should serve but one noble and eternal purpose: to bring forth the *Gesamtkunstwerk* and thereby to realize the idea of true German art which expresses the innermost being of the nation. Interestingly Wagner states emphatically that he has not yet achieved this ideal with what he has hitherto created, and that clear recognition of the fundamental facts is only the first step towards reaching this goal.

It is astounding that Wagner believed all this with fervent conviction. Despite his tremendous, highly developed intellect and his all-embracing spirit, Wagner is so totally emotional in his character that he is incapable of analytic thought: he cannot examine given facts objectively. The starting point of his analysis is a preconceived idea: he has settled on his aim, and therefore all the results of his researches must, with logical necessity, lead towards this aim. His entire theory with all its historical and aesthetic inferences has only one purpose, namely to build the platform on which he himself can stand as the first true music dramatist in history, creator of a work which strives from the misery of a dissolute era to the high ideal of pure art. This may be megalomania, but he needed this belief in order to achieve what, in fact, he *did* achieve. *Der Ring des Nibelungen*, *Die Meistersinger* could only grow out of the unshakeable belief in his mission. In his young days his ambition could still be lured by thoughts of an operatic success, but such trivial aims he had left far behind him: now he could only create when he was convinced that he was doing something which no-one before him had ever done or even envisaged.

But in order to fulfil his mission, and in order to obtain the necessary understanding and the requisite material necessities, one condition must be categorically enforced: opera must be abolished—opera, this shallow and frivolous entertainment of a frivolous and shallow public, this opera for which public means are ever available. These funds must be channelled towards the achievement of noble objectives—to wit, his own. The quotation from the epilogue in the first edition of the *Ring* text (cf. pp. 82f.) has already made this train of thought quite obvious. This *idée fixe* of Wagner's, this opera hatred of his, was also rooted in an emotional background. Because of such trivial operas his own works were not performed in Paris; there he had to work his fingers to the bone, arranging the shabby music of Halévy, Donizetti; in Dresden he had to stand by and suffer the execrations of Flotow, Hérold, Donizetti, Bellini to remain in the repertoire—worse, he even had to conduct them. The consuming desire of the young artist to see his work performed became the soil from which grew the unconditional demand to rule as an absolute monarch in that temple in which an audience avid for entertainment was daily prepared to cheer the products of Meyerbeer, Verdi, Gounod, competing with whom he could only regard as a further humiliation. Hence his *ceterum censeo:* opera had inflicted sufferings on him, therefore opera had to be destroyed.

To a large extent these totalitarian claims of his theory explain the open hostility with which Wagner was received by contemporary critics and many contemporary musicians. He had always been able to take the ordinary public by storm and without resistance. In Vienna, the home of his best-hated critical opponent, Eduard Hanslick, a suburban theatre created a sensation with *Tannhäuser* and played to full houses, whilst at the *Hofoper* no work of the "barricade merchant" (as he was called in allusion to his revolutionary activities on the barricades of Dresden) was as yet allowed to be as much as considered. Even later, when *Lohengrin* was performed there, no seat was to be had for days on end whenever the work was on the programme. Enough said: these facts show how little damage music critics could do to Wagner and how much he himself over-estimated their influence. Perhaps he also over-estimated their maliciousness. His critics—from Hanslick downwards, who at least was musically educated—may have been insensitive and unappreciative, but they could all read. Anyone who was not prepared to follow Wagner through thick and thin *a priori* could hardly fail to reject theories such as his. Wagner himself ascribed the hostility of the press to another cause, namely his pamphlet *Das Judentum in der Musik* ("Judaism in Music"), but the reason for this attitude probably had its root in the same bad conscience which prevented him from signing this treatise with his own name when he published it in 1850. In principle it is an attack on the two most famous and influential musicians of his time, Mendelssohn and Meyerbeer, whom in this simple manner he brings down to a common denominator—although he himself admits that they had little in common. If one takes into consideration that Wagner, never and under no circumstances, would give any of his contemporaries their due, be it as a composer or as a poet (he turned on Schumann and Brahms as impartially as on Hebbel and Grillparzer) it seems quite likely that, perhaps only subconsciously, he was egged on by the chance of putting two such dangerous rivals *hors de combat* with one single blow. With this pamphlet, and long before Treitschke, Wagner became the father of cultural anti-semitism. As in his dissertation on the aesthetic, the reasons which he propounds are pretexts which have only one purpose: to prove a preconceived idea, in this case that a Jew is of alien origin—and consequently incapable of making European or German culture and its way of thinking

completely his own. In the case of Mendelssohn, whose outstanding talent he freely admits, the result is an interesting and
technically indisputable description of trifling content. With
Meyerbeer, by contrast, the composition of operas is a business
enterprise, clever speculation on success, a striving for effect
at any price, for effect without cause. It is difficult to escape
the impression that Wagner's later and ever more ruthlessly
accentuated anti-semitism only gained fresh fuel from the
sensational impact which this pamphlet had, and that action
and reaction caused an ever-increasing intensity of this attitude.
Be this as it may, he tended to see a Jew in every critic—for
example Hanslick, who was not Jewish—and to suspect every
Jew of stirring up the press against him, for instance, Meyerbeer.
His wife Cosima was his faithful disciple in this respect, and
many years later she turned Lenin into a Jew because she
disapproved of him.

Since Wagner had descended into the arena of controversy
and publicistic polemics, not only did his name become a pivot
point of all politico-artistic discussions, but he himself had
become an object of controversy and remained one for the rest
of his life. With his irresistible desire to give public utterance
about everything which happened to move him, he was an
aggressor just as often as he was the attacked, and he was
constantly involved in some quarrel or other. In a letter to
Cornelius from Triebschen he expressed himself on this state of
affairs, obviously with some satisfaction to his vanity:

> There is not much to be said about me, especially as so much
> is said about me in other quarters. Anyone pondering from
> morning till night how to go about it to create as much
> scandal as possible about himself could not have done better
> by one hair's breadth. I think people are envying me my lot.
> Brahms for instance doesn't seem to have any luck at all in
> this respect.

How badly he knew Brahms if he credited him with such
exhibitionistic tendencies! In a marginal note about Wagner,
Hanslick—who, musically speaking, was a philistine but
otherwise quite witty—quotes what Hebbel said about Schiller:

"This holy man! Destiny has ever cursed him, and ever Schiller has blessed destiny!" and he adds: "Destiny has also cursed the composer of *Lohengrin* for long, but he cursed destiny even more." Incidentally, Hanslick was considerably more objective in his criticisms than Wagner in his. The one thing to which he objected more than anything else was Wagner's claim that he was of sole and unique importance, but he never denied Wagner his greatness. In his criticism of *Parsifal* he wrote: "We know very well that Wagner is the greatest of all living opera composers, and in Germany he is the only one of whom one can seriously speak in an historical sense." He continued, not without a note of sadness: "In this day and age anyone who does not compose in the Wagnerian manner is as good as lost— and anyone who does, is doubly lost."

Perhaps no one has characterized the duality of Wagner's nature more aptly than the Alsatian writer Edouard Schuré, who met Wagner in Munich at the time of the *Tristan* performance and later was his guest in Triebschen and Bayreuth:

> Looking at him one could see in his face two persons: from the front a Faust, in profile a Mephistopheles. The fullness of that protean nature was dazzling—incandescent, wilful, extravagant in every respect, and yet wonderfully in balance because of his all-embracing intellect. . . . The frankness with which he bared his inner nature, the qualities and defects which he unveiled unashamedly, was of magical attraction to some, repellent to others.

One of Wagner's most prominent friends, the philosopher Friedrich Nietzsche, came to know both, the attraction as well as the repulsion. After the first Bayreuth Festival he was converted from a Paul into a Saul, from one of Wagner's most ardent admirers into one of his most irreconcilable opponents. With penetrating vision he had recognized Wagner's weaknesses, although possibly hurt pride may have played its part too. Wagner could never see more in his highly-gifted young friend than a useful propagandist in the service of his, Wagner's, cause. He could not comprehend that Nietzsche had the ambition to accomplish something worthwhile on his own account, and Wagner replied to Nietzsche's dissertation "Socrates and Greek Tragedy" with the well-meaning advice: "Now, you show what philology is good for and help me to bring about that great Renaissance in which Plato embraces Homer— and Homer, filled with Platonic ideas, now really becomes the very greatest Homer." It is easy to see the estimation in which he held himself, but when it came to egotism Nietzsche was his peer. As a representative of a younger generation he was the first true anti-romantic, the first who withdrew from the romantic chaos and romantic sentimental wallowings, and it must have been this which led to the parting of the ways with Wagner. It must be admitted that he made his later remarks about Wagner, in which he was seething with hatred, only a matter of a few years before his mental collapse, which may explain their excessive irritation.

For an ever-restless spirit like Wagner theoretical speculation was an escape from the menacing feel of emptiness when his creative urge failed him. Once his creative urge returned he was happy to leave all ponderings, writings and preaching behind him. When the *Ring* began to take shape he wrote to Röckel:

> My literary work only gave evidence of my lack of freedom as an artist: I only wrote these things under the greatest of compulsions, and there was nothing further from my mind than to write "books" . . . but now my literary period is over and done with: I would rather be dead than continue with it. . . .

Yet in a later period of artistic rebirth after a prolonged creative pause, when he was composing *Meistersinger*, he was unable to resist the temptation of meddling in politics again, although he had burnt his fingers once before. Of course, the crisis of 1866 gave him ample opportunity of voicing his opinions in front of the King, politicians, publicists and all, nor could he forbear, as a gesture of protest, to send to the Bavarian President of Cabinet, Prinz Hohenlohe, the final chapter of his dissertation *Deutsche Kunst und deutsche Politik* (cf. p. 95) which had been confiscated and publication of which had been banned by the King. However, this final experience seems to have brought him to his senses, and never again did he engage himself in Bavarian politics.

All the more did he occupy himself from the very beginning of the Bayreuth project with the immense problems of its realization. Fortunately the composition of *Götterdämmerung* had at least been completed in draft form when Wagner entered the critical stage of the whole enterprise with his own move to Bayreuth, when on top of all worries of a financial nature he also personally took upon himself the nerve-racking sisyphean labours of a theatre manager. Bayreuth was the last and most memorable achievement of Wagner the Man of Action. Strangely enough it also brought him into superficial contact with that other great man of action of his time, Bismarck, who once received him in Berlin when the first preparations were made for the Festival. It was their one and only personal meeting. Later Wagner wrote to Bismarck and enclosed a brochure about the *Festspielhaus*, but the Chancellor of the German *Reich* did not reply: apparently the idea of a rejuvenation of the German nation via the theatre did not appeal to him. Wagner never had another good word to say about Bismarck.

2

MONEY, DEBTS, LUXURY

OF THE MANY peculiarities of Wagner's character his almost pathological extravagance takes first place. It is part and parcel of his unusual constitution that every trait in his character is super-dimensional; but his relationship to money is so erratic that some special consideration must be given to this aspect. He himself must have felt this when, in a letter to his Dresden doctor and friend Pusinelli, he broached the subject at a time (1870) when, thanks to the largesse of King Ludwig, he could have been living without any material worries. In this letter he wrote about the main obstacles in the course of his life:

My lack of possessions has always been the very worst. What anyone inherits may be much or little, yet it gives the necessary independence to a person who is striving for something which is serious and genuine: with all my determination, and especially in my sphere of activity, the necessity of having to earn money for one's living is an utter curse. Many great ones have already experienced this and have foundered in consequence. I am convinced that even moderate possessions would have made me quite stable in the external course of my life and would have put me far beyond all this restlessness. The completely contrary conditions, however, made me indifferent to the value of money, as though I had known that actually I would never "earn" money for my living. As a result I have had to suffer incredibly, whilst in all other respects the trends of my life have been ideal.

This lack of inherited assets has been shared by just about all of Wagner's famous precursors and contemporaries with only two exceptions: Mendelssohn and Meyerbeer; and apparently

Wagner held this against them as much as he did their fame. Let us leave the question open whether under any given circumstances he would ever have been capable of living an unassuming and modest life, but there can be no doubt that the struggle for mere existence which he had to fight from early youth had a decisive influence on his attitude towards all things material. His lust for life, the intensity of his desires and wants, taught him early how to get what he needed. At first it was his brothers, sisters, in-laws, friends who had to pay up, but later there was literally no one who could enter the sphere of his personality and be safe from his predatory acts. With the irresistible eloquence which he had at his command he had learnt—by demanding, begging, flattering—to get money out of any pocket in which there was money to be found, and his requirements rose steadily in proportion to the growth of his importance, his self-conceit, and the demands resulting from these. Different personalities have different reactions. Haydn, Beethoven, Brahms, Verdi had experienced poverty during their youth, and this made them modest and unassuming in their personal requirements for the rest of their lives. In Wagner's case the result was the opposite: it boundlessly stimulated and increased his desires for the good things in life, just as in his manner of reacting every impact invariably led to an impassioned counter-impact. The privations of the Paris years turned him into an epicurean for life; as a result of the constant material uncertainty and threat during his exile and the years of restless roamings, his yearning for luxury took on positively sybaritic proportions; when finally he was safe and without any immediate worries, the feeling of dependence on the whims of his King convinced him that now his dignity could only be properly upheld by a princely sovereignty of his own—with, of course, an equally princely way of life. Bayreuth became a Court, he only travelled in his private Pullman coach, and on holidays in Italy the Wagner family of seven needed eight servants.

Three circumstances are equally noteworthy in Wagner's attitude to financial matters: his enormous and ever increasing needs, the way in which he got the money, and his behaviour towards his creditors. In all three respects his conduct was unusual, and that is putting it mildly. Any form of reticence

as regards his requirements did not even come under consideration. Whatever appeared to be desirable at the moment he had
to have, and immediately at that, regardless of costs. To obtain
funds he always made use of pawn-shops: he pawned whatever
valuables he possessed, but preferably the receipts expected
from works not yet written. It must be admitted that his
expectations in that direction came true later—but only much,
much later. During the days of his financial operations of this
type, which initially were based on those works of his which
actually existed, only an uninhibited optimist or a confidence
trickster could possibly assert, when taking up such loans, that
incomes were assured and imminent, and offer them as a
guarantee. By taking the risk of such a course his primary aim
was to shift the immediate worries on to whoever lent the money.
In the very beginnings of his career, in Magdeburg, he had laid
the foundations for his progressively worsening indebtedness.
So he wrote to his friend Theodor Apel, who was well-off and to
whom he already owed a few hundred *Taler*:

> I am not asking for a present, but do buy the receipts of my
> opera! If you have faith in me, you are just the one who has
> nothing to fear; I estimate that it will bring one hundred
> *Taler*: will you give me that? It is an honest deal, and I only
> turn to you because I feel justified in believing that you have
> the greatest faith in my success. If I do not receive the money
> during this month, I cannot show my face here any longer.

The income which he expected was the net receipts from a
second performance of *Das Liebesverbot*, which was to have been
given as a charity performance for him. But it never took place.
Once he had received the loan, the obligations into which he had
entered were wiped from his memory. Demands for repayment
he ignored whenever possible; when they became too urgent he
covered them by a new loan, and only in cases of extreme
emergency did he dip into his own pocket.

Wagner's ever-growing need, his complete unconcern in
matters of obtaining money, and his unwillingness to repay his
debts all have a common background: his unshakeable
conviction that the world had a sacred and bounden duty to

keep him in a fashion appropriate to his standing; that the greatness and importance of what he had accomplished entitled him to an equivalent compensation, and that everyone who was in a position to contribute to his justified demands in this regard was only doing his duty and did not deserve any further consideration. His suppliers he dealt with in a similar spirit by obtaining from them on credit whatever he could get. He blithely signed promissory notes and IOUs and regarded it a malicious arrangement in our social order that some day they fall due. To earn money was beneath his dignity. That was only for the small-minded and the philistines. For him it was suffi- cient to spend it, and just as he despised the philistines, so he despised the money which he extracted from them. He therefore always did his best to get rid of it again as speedily as possible.

All this was not the result of logical thought on his part, but of emotionally-rooted impulses which were irresistible because they were completely irrational. There are countless remarks in Wagner's letters which spring from such emotions. It is only necessary to glance through his letters to Liszt—who, with infinite kindness and patience, had given him again and again as much as he could—and the following is a small selection.

23 June 1848; Liszt had given up his activities as a concert pianist and had settled in Weimar on a considerably smaller salary than that with which Wagner could not make do in Dresden:

> You told me recently that you had locked up your piano for a while; I take it that you have become a banker. I am badly off, and I had the sudden idea that you might be able to help me. I myself have undertaken the publication of my three operas, for which I have borrowed the capital here and there. Now all these debts are being called in, and I cannot hold out for another week. . . . All in all it is a matter of 5000 *Taler*. . . . Can you get me the money? Do you have it, or is there someone who has it and would give it for your sake? Would it not be very interesting if you were to become the publisher-proprietor of my operas? My dear Liszt, with that money you will redeem me out of my bondage! Am I worth that much to you as a serf?

Six years later, from Zürich:

> In the course of the next three months I now expect my opera revenues for this year; the indications are that they will be very good, and I hope that once and for all they will get me out of this last fix. The least I can expect is a sum of 1000 *Taler*. So, to whoever lends them to me I will, with a clean conscience, give a promissory note for a term of three months.

Yet another two years later:

> I ask you, even better, could you make me a present of the 1000 francs? And would it be possible for you during each of the next two years to make over to me an allowance of a similar amount? [And regarding Liszt's advice to accept an offer from America . . .] Good Lord, sums such as those which I could "earn" (??) in America people should *give* to me, without demanding anything else than just that which I *am* doing, and which is the best I *can* do. Apart from that it is much more in my character to spend 60,000 francs in six months than to "earn" them, for this I cannot do at all: it is not my business to "earn money", but it would be the business of my admirers to give me as much money as I need to keep me in good cheer and create something worthwhile.

Then again:

> I declare that, having lived in exile for ten years, I have got used to it, and it is not amnesty which I consider the greatest boon, but the guarantee of means which would assure me of a carefree and comfortable existence for the rest of my life. [And regarding his demands . . .] If again I am to plunge into the ocean of artistic imagination in order to keep myself satisfied in this illusory world, then at least my imagination must be held and my fantasy must be assisted—then I cannot live like a dog, I cannot sleep on straw and drink raw spirits; somehow I must feel myself flattered if my spirit is to

succeed in the cruelly difficult task of creating an as yet non-existent world.

From a conversation with Wagner, Frau Eliza Wille of Mariafeld made a note of his words:

> My make-up is different, I have irritable nerves: I simply must have beauty, splendour, light! The world owes me whatever I need. I cannot exist in a miserable organist's post like your Master Bach!

It appears he took it amiss that his friend did not care for him better, as shown by a letter to Ferdinand Heine in Dresden:

> As for Liszt—this has also become apparent—he is incapable of maintaining me, for he himself is constantly embarrassed financially. . . . He is a magnificent man with excellent characteristics, and he has great sympathy for me, but he cannot realize the true essence of my artistic nature, and it will ever remain alien to him. That is the root of the matter. Enough of this. For more than three months I have been living on a few hundred guilders which have been advanced to me by a local friend who, however, did his utmost with this loan. After the end of this month I simply do not know what I am to live on. This would not be so terrible if it were only myself, but it worries me very much as regards my wife, even though in the end and in many respects I shall always remain an insoluble riddle to her.

23 March 1856; Liszt was highly embarrassed and virtually apologized:

> At long last I can inform you that you will receive 1000 francs early in May. . . . On several occasions I have told you of my difficult financial situation which simply came about because my earlier savings had to go to the decent upkeep of my mother and my three children, and I myself have to live on my *Kapellmeister*'s salary (1000 *Taler* annually plus 300 *Taler* as a special gratuity for the Court Concerts). . . .

So please do not hold it against me, my dear Richard, if I cannot agree to your proposition, for at the moment I cannot enter any regularly recurring obligations. If my circumstances were to improve later, which is not beyond the bounds of possibility, it will be my greatest pleasure to alleviate your position.

But you cannot put Wagner off as easily as that! It is Liszt's business to see to it that several German Princes will band together in their willingness to provide him with an annual pension, which—

if it is to correspond completely to their purpose as well as my admittedly somewhat sensitive and not quite everyday needs, would have to run to at least two or three thousand *Taler*. I do not blush to name such a sum: on the one hand I have the experience that just I, as I happen to be (and also, perhaps, the way in which I envisage my works) cannot manage comfortably on less; on the other I have watched how artists like Mendelssohn [here he goes again!], although actually he was already wealthy enough, were granted no smaller honorary annuities—and from one single source at that.

Very few of Wagner's friendships could withstand such egotism without coming to grief. The person who suffered most under it was Minna with her deeply rooted bourgeois feelings—and Wagner was scared of her and preferred not to let her know about his minor debts: "When the money from Vienna comes in, please pay 100 francs to Müller (it was all he had). The other 100 francs I have borrowed from Semper, and I herewith confess it with trepidation. Semper is not so hard pressed, but you may offer them to him also."

That was in Zürich amidst modest conditions, when he had but a small, well-run household. The vertiginous rise in his expenditure and the all but maniacal haste with which he threw money out of the window date from his stay in Paris at the time of the *Tannhäuser* episode. This in turn led to the terrible crisis in Vienna when he had to take to his heels and was finally saved by the intervention of King Ludwig. But from then onwards his expenditure could still be plotted as a steeply rising graph. When he returned from Russia and set up an opulent hearth in Vienna-Penzing with the takings which had resulted from that journey, he also began his business relationships with the milliner Berta Goldwag who later became notorious through journalistic indiscretion and the publication of Wagner's letters to her. In Vienna he remained indebted to her for 1500 florins, and later he paid them back only by scanty instalments. Then he had her come specially to Munich and bring goods—brocade, satin, velvet, silk, lace—to the value of 10,000 florins so that he could furnish his new home to his taste. Later, in Triebschen, it was a similar story. As an anxious friend, Peter Cornelius who visited him there was worried again:

> Now again he has sunk a heap of money here, has rebuilt and decorated, and when you see such an aviary full of gold pheasants and other rare birds you cannot help thinking: heaven help us, how much must the man have paid for all that? Add to this the cultivation of a few acres of park lands and vegetable gardens—eight servants or so at a modest estimate—a gig and horse . . . Enough! I only know one thing: one day I shall be sitting together with Wagner over a bottle of wine or beer and a very frugal meal, when he will no longer have either the King or Cosima. Then he will tell me many things, and at times he will become highly vehement.

Ernest Newman has calculated that within four years (1864–1867) Wagner had received 130,000 florins—a quarter million *Mark*—from the Treasury of the King's Cabinet. Small surprise that this caused much comment. Wahnfried cost another fortune. From Bayreuth Wagner wrote to Schott, his publishers:

> You would do me an extraordinary favour if you could let me have immediately and in advance the 10,000 francs stipulated for your purchase of the copyright of the *Götterdämmerung* score. . . . I have ear-marked that sum to complete and furnish my house, and as things stand my hands are tied if I cannot dispose of those funds. . . .

Schott paid up. A few months later Wagner came back again: "I need 10,000 guilders in order to complete my house and garden." In return he offered the publishers six orchestral works which he intended to compose during the next few years, and he concluded: "My proposition, my wish, my request may be somewhat out of the ordinary, but it is Franz Schott to whom I direct it and, after all, it is Richard Wagner who does so." Schott paid up again. Wagner never got round to writing those promised orchestral works, but he made it up to the publishers by demanding from them 100,000 *Mark* for the publication rights of *Parsifal* (not the stage rights—he kept those for himself). Schott agreed the terms, since they could deduct their advances from that sum.

Thanks to the memoirs of Wendelin Weissheimer, who was constantly in Wagner's company during the Vienna concerts in the winter of 1861/62, we know of another pretty and typically Wagnerian episode:

Wagner had been staying at his hotel for two months. He was still hoping for the payment which was to be made to him after the first performance of *Tristan*, but it did not arrive— the proprietor became worried and sent him one bill after the other. . . . When one evening, together with Tausig, I went to visit him, he was full of woe and bemoaned his miserable position. Full of sympathy we listened to him and sat on the sofa in deep depression, while he was pacing up and down in nervous haste. Suddenly he stopped dead and said: "Ah, now I know what is missing and what I need." He ran to the door and rang the bell loudly. The waiter finally appeared, slowly and with hesitation, for these people soon know which way the wind is blowing, and he was no less amazed than we were when Wagner ordered: "Will you bring us immediately two bottles of champagne on ice!" "For God's sake, in this situation!" we cried out when the waiter had left again. But he gave us a fervent lecture on the absolute necessity of champagne especially in desperate situations—only champagne could help one to overcome such embarrassments. . . . If you associated with Wagner you went from surprise to surprise. When I entered his room next morning he showed me 1000 guilders which the Empress had sent him, presumably at the instigation of Dr Standhartner [Wagner's friend and personal physician to Empress Elisabeth].

Talking of champagne, let us just mention by the way that when Wagner's Penzing home was compulsorily auctioned off, the contents included one hundred bottles of that precious liquid. There is no record, however, of whether Wagner had ever paid for them.

Wagner's last letter, written two days before his death, was addressed to Angelo Neumann, the enterprising impresario who was then touring all European capitals with *Der Ring des Nibelungen* and thereby earning sizeable royalties for Wagner. The letter finishes with a request for money.

3

THE POET-COMPOSER

ONLY ONE GENERATION before Wagner a literary education was still something exceptional amongst musicians. Probably Weber was the first great composer who could also voice his views regarding the problems of his art as a writer, and after him Schumann, Berlioz, Liszt. Wagner's case is completely different. According to information from his own pen the literary activities of his youthful years preceded the musical. In any case it is certain that for the whole duration of his life they took an important place side by side with his work as a composer, and very soon—and without contradiction—his contemporaries accorded him the title of "Poet-Composer", and this not only from the pro-Wagnerian factions who were quite happy to pair him with Goethe as a poet and with Beethoven as a musician. Wagner's innate dramatic talent is incredible, and in the realm of opera this talent can be considered unique. It must be admitted that even the greatest masters of opera—Gluck, Mozart, Weber, Rossini, Verdi—sometimes made apparently inevitable errors over the choice and dramatic moulding of their subjects. This never happened to Wagner. He had the gift of fashioning every subject which came under his hand into a vital dramatic form and, as it seems, without the least difficulty. He designed such dramatic sketches in his head while hiking, and the elaboration and transposition into verse was achieved with the same effortless elegance. This rare and extraordinary facility had the result that all his works, from *Rienzi* to *Parsifal*, are shaped with such an assured ease that from their very first production on stage there could never be one iota of doubt about their effectiveness, and all of them, with the possible exception of *Rienzi* with its largely very questionable musical worth, have remained in the repertoire in the opera houses of the world with undiminished vitality. This tremendous accomplishment alone gives Wagner a very special place amongst all music dramatists.

As a dramatist Wagner was remarkably precocious—a precocity which is already noticeable in his early operas, *Die Feen* and *Das Liebesverbot*—but by contrast he matured very much more slowly as a composer. In those two early operas there is hardly a phrase to be found which one would feel tempted to ascribe to Wagner, and the same applies to the other works of his youthful days which have become known. There are a piano sonata, a symphony (which Wagner performed on the last Christmas Day of his life in Venice, cf. p. 104), four overtures composed in Leipzig, Magdeburg and Königsberg (*König Enzio*, *Christoph Columbus*, *Polonia* and *Rule Britannia*) but they are all the works of a beginner—of a sound, decently trained, mediocre talent. There are many instances of comparison. Even if one disregards miracles such as Mozart or Mendelssohn, there is hardly another outstanding talent which, one way or another, has not given some sort of proof of true individuality of invention or expression at the age of twenty. This applies to Beethoven as it does to Schubert, to Weber, Schumann, Chopin, Brahms. But young Wagner is not merely uncertain: his style swings undecidedly as a pendulum between dubious models of all kinds, with only occasional reminiscences of Beethoven and Weber clothed in an embarrassed apology. Wagner's youth coincides with a nadir of general taste, which is clearly recognizable by the fact that he himself lacked a true sense of style.

It would take us too far afield to do more than brush the reasons which, during the life time of Beethoven and Schubert, had contributed to this decline of music and, in particular, opera. The arts are a very sensitive barometer for the conditions of an epoch. Throughout the whole of Europe an over-bred, over-cultured society had been ploughed under by the events of the French Revolution and the Napoleonic Wars, and a new public, naïve and primitive in its tastes, now filled the theatres. The best evidence of the social set-up of that era can be found in the novels of Stendhal and Balzac. The splendiferous and sparkling Rossini—the most representative of all opera composers of that time who, at the apex of his fortunes, transferred the arena of his activities to Paris—was followed by Donizetti and Bellini as the most successful composers through whom vocal virtuosity became the very life and soul of Italian opera. Then, with Rossini's last opera *Guillaume Tell*, the door was opened for that great historico-romantic panorama for which the way had already been paved by Spontini and which now—with Meyerbeer, Hérold, Halévy—burst into full bloom. It was that sort of opera which Wagner encountered on German stages when he began his career as an operatic conductor. The German operas which tried to hold their own—those of Weber, Spohr, Marschner, Lortzing—had much to contend with in opposing the facile, scintillating French and Italian imports.

Today, viewing all this from the distance of more than a century, the light of Rossini's works outshines all the operas of his day and age. Bellini and his successor Donizetti still have much that is genuine, and for that reason lovable, in their Italian tradition and singability, so that one is inclined to pardon much primitiveness of form and design; one even forgives them that their orchestration is based on a pattern and simply enjoys their positive traits: Bellini's far-flung, vigorous melodic line, Donizetti's vital rhythm and incomparable humour. A similarly genuine style—and indeed often brilliantly comic elements—are also to be found in the French *opéra comique*, especially in the case of Boïeldieu and Auber, both of whom incidentally were highly esteemed by Wagner. But it is difficult to find so much as a trace of sympathy for *grand opéra*, whose main representative was Meyerbeer. It is true that he knew how to compose and had an undeniable instinct for dramatic gesture, but this goes hand in hand for much of the time with such arid invention and so much empty bathos that all the wealth of pomp and scenic machinery unfortunately deserves Wagner's description: "effect without cause".

Nevertheless, it must be admitted that there is little in Wagner's *Rienzi* score which could not be by Meyerbeer, and in *Les Huguenots* there are passages which are better than the best of *Rienzi*. Hardly anywhere in *Rienzi*—an opera which, in its dimensions, must be termed colossal—is anything to be found which is really Wagnerian, and even such a soaring and resplendent item as the *Santo spirito cavaliere* is a cliché pure and simple. The phraseology of French opera dominates in every detail, and mannered melodic cadences *à la* Meyerbeer such as

are repeated *ad nauseam*. This type of cadence continues to haunt *Der fliegende Holländer* as well as *Tannhäuser* and *Lohengrin*, and at long last *Lohengrin* bids us farewell with a variant of that selfsame phrase:

sein Rit - ter, ich bin Lo-hen-grin ge- nannt.

Without doubt one of Wagner's reasons for his later revolt against the operatic style of the time was his objection to a heroically overcome original sin. Of course *Rienzi* belongs to this type of everyday opera libretto, for despite its brilliant and taut attitude to stage requirements it falls into the same category with all its conventional *dramatis personae* and conflicts. Nevertheless in the whole gamut of Meyerbeer there is not a single libretto of the same order, and this is the advantage which Wagner the Dramatist had over Wagner the Composer. In later years Wagner had little affection for this early work of his and avoided it. In reality, by then he had little left in common with the composer of that music: he had found another self and a language of his own, and much though this developed and became refined during the long course of his artistic life it still remained the same language, the same impressive and expressive organ of the soul of an artist who could sublimate his earthly and spiritual experiences.

What is so extraordinary is the suddenness with which Wagner himself became aware of his wing-span when the conception of *Der fliegende Holländer* matured within him. As in his emotional life, his creativity is an expression of unbridled and impulsive forces within himself. Immediately after completing *Rienzi* he turned to this vision which he had long borne in his subconscious, and in the following summer the music broke forth in full spate. It was the reaction of his creative urge after the difficult experiences of the last few years, which had had a cumulative effect. The escape from Riga, the peril at sea, the misery in Paris, the humiliation of a debtors' prison—all these impressions coalesced into a trauma which, as has been mentioned before, influenced his spiritual life for ever, just as at that time unenvisaged creative forces which had been slumbering within him were suddenly liberated. *Der fliegende Holländer* is not an invention, but something which has been experienced. The most gripping element of this work is the reality of its utterance. The storm which whips up the music is not a stage effect. The Norwegian seamen, the spinning room, the ghost ship are facts which have been seen, have been felt, are real. And in the character of the Dutchman, longing for salvation, there is so much of Wagner himself, that restless, homeless wanderer, just as in many of his heroes we can find traces of a self-portrait. In the subsidiary characters and their music much is conventional: Daland, that prosaically benevolent father, could appear in any French opera; small wonder that his music sounds like Meyerbeer. And Erik, that unfortunate spurned lover, has a lot of lacrimose Marschner about him whenever he gets lyrical. Nevertheless, when he tells of his dream which Senta shares "as though in a magnetic sleep" we are captivated by a breathtaking tension—it is a new musical language of an intensity which had never been heard before, and which gives the whole subsequent drama a focal point of concentration. There is another such focal point which comprehends the whole of the drama: the scene in the third act when Norwegians and Dutchmen meet, when reality collides with the world of spooks. Even Wagner's fantastic vision has never created anything more gripping. Of course, Senta, this emblem of true, devoted, sacrificial femininity, is a wishful dream like so many of Wagner's other heroines and, in common with all of them, it is so difficult to find an ideal Senta because the tender beauty and the dramatic heroism of the character somehow will not merge. With *Der fliegende Holländer* Wagner began his *via dolorosa*, his life-long search for the ideal interpreter. In straight theatre there are also character types for which the young actor must be trained, but in opera the character is of far greater import because it must identify itself with type of voice and type of vocal character. Hence the well-known types of older opera whose chief deficiency is the fact that the librettist has tried to make his subject tailor-made for each of his actors: one a juvenile high soprano, another a dulcetly-fluting tenor, and then of course a menacing, black-bearded bass whom every experienced opera-goer could identify from his first entrance as the villain of the piece. With his innate sensitivity *against* operatic tradition Wagner, from the very beginning, had created characters which transcended the conventional operatic style and presented new problems of production. What he could not alter were the purely physical conditions of singing. A good actor, according to his stature and nature, can cope with any part whatsoever to the best of his talents, and his vocal capabilities are relatively unimportant. It is quite possible to imagine a completely introvert Hamlet, played by an actor of very limited vocal means. In opera it is different, and especially in Wagner with his passionately and relentlessly weaving and resounding orchestra and the uncompromising accentuation demanded by his declamatory style. What Senta is supposed to sing—or Venus, Brünnhilde, Ortrud or Kundry, to mention just a few—cannot be sung without a certain amount of physical exertion, which in turn necessitates a certain robust physical constitution. The same applies to Wagner's heroic tenors: Tannhäuser, Lohengrin, Tristan, Siegfried. The result is that, thanks to Wagner's style, in the ranks of the conventional types of singers we now have two more: the highly dramatic heroic tenor with the neck of a bull and the muscles of a wrestler, and the super-dimensional bosomy dramatic soprano. This is the practical result of idealistic demands, one of the many symptoms of Wagner's grandiose but utopian vision.

This visionary lack of inhibitions is in direct opposition to Wagner's practical experience, but it is that same lack of inhibitions which led to *Tristan* when he wanted to compose a simple, easily performable opera, and it is at one and the same time one of Wagner's tremendous qualities and also the source of the many problems which his works present. The vision of the dramatist finds its sublimation in a musical idea which seems to embrace the essence of the entire work, a tone symbol of the greatest pregnancy and memorability:

This opening of the *Holländer* Overture—and every Wagner work contains material of such spontaneity—is overpowering and as inescapable as an outbreak of molten lava, for Wagner's inspiration can best be compared with the uncontrollable phenomena of nature.

Perhaps it is permissible to digress briefly from the particular to the general. This generality is the inspiration (as this mysterious act of invention is customarily called) which is the basis of every musical composition. There are two different principles of this process of inspiration which, borrowing my terminology from the realm of nature, I would like to term the volcanic and the sedimentary. In the former case the inspiration comes as a sudden, intuitive flash of a creative fantasy virtually unaffected by the critically observing consciousness which, so to speak, has merely the task of solidifying the intangible substance which otherwise could so easily dissolve into thin air. In contrast the sedimentary product, like the precipitate of a saturated solution, settles very slowly in the depths of consciousness as a precious material, a process which may take a long period of time. This act of creation is dependent on the instinct and the experience of an artist who has learnt to wait until the crystallization has reached perfection and the material is of ideal consistency.

Most artists know both these forms of inspiration, but in each individual the one or other usually predominates. Wagner would appear to be an extreme case of almost entirely volcanic production, just as Brahms in almost all aspects seems first and foremost to belong to the sedimentary category—and in Beethoven's sketches one can discover highly interesting combinations of both types of inspiration. It is hardly necessary to stress that in both cases an infinite amount of artistic labour still remains to be done before a work of art has taken shape out of the inspiration, before an edifice has risen from bare bricks and mortar. Nor is it necessary to point out that at every stage of the execution creative fantasy plays an indispensable and decisive part.

With Wagner each inspiration was a violent eruption, but he also had the limitless patience to wait for it. Very rarely was he granted an easy and spontaneous idea. Something had to grip him in the very depth of his soul for him to be able to write anything at all. He himself defined poetry as the male, music as the female partner of a musico-dramatic conception, and this definition certainly applies to him: the musician Wagner had to have a poetical concept in order to become productive, and without the poet the composer could never have existed. In actual fact he was always denied the sheer joy of carefree improvisation. In this respect the Entry of the Guests on the Wartburg, which has already been mentioned, is an exception fostered by particularly happy and productive circumstances. His other occasional compositions—Album Leaves and the like—are almost embarrassingly paltry and by themselves would never lead anyone to believe that they were written by a great composer. Three major works of that type, three marches dating from his late period—*Huldigungsmarsch*, *Kaisermarsch*, *Festmarsch*—have long been forgotten, and justly so. The only occasional work worthy of Wagner's name is the *Siegfried-Idyll* which he composed in 1870 for Cosima's birthday. It is deeply rooted in the mood and emotional world of *Siegfried*, and almost all the thematic material of the *Idyll* can be traced back to the last act of that music drama. Of his songs there are basically only the five that he wrote to poems by Mathilde Wesendonck which are of any interest, and the two finest of them, *Träume* and *Im Treibhaus*, Wagner used again in his *Tristan* on which he was working at the time. An orchestral work from Paris days, *Eine Faust-Ouvertüre*, has its significance since, composed one year before *Der fliegende Holländer*, it presages that style in a curious manner. What this serious and staunch work lacks is true inspiration. There is no getting away from it: Wagner was only a musical dramatist, and only as poet-composer could he rise to his full stature.

At the time of the *Holländer* Wagner did not yet regard himself as a poet. This is indicated in a letter which he wrote on 30 January 1844 to Carl Gaillard, the only Berlin critic who had written favourably about the *Holländer*. In addition this letter also contains cogent remarks concerning his attitude at that time to the problem of opera and drama—an attitude which, of course, changed radically later:

I cannot say that I have an over-high opinion of my *métier* as poet and confess that I only took it up as a matter of necessity: no decent texts were offered to me, and so I had to write them myself. Now, however, it would be impossible for me to set someone else's libretto to music for the following simple reason: with me it is not the case that I pick on some subject or other, set it to verse and then start thinking about suitable music for it. In this type of procedure I would have to face the evil of having to get enraptured twice over, which is impossible. My way of creating is different: first of all no subject can attract me except one which immediately conjures up not only a poetic but also a musical vision within me. Before I start writing even the very first line I am already intoxicated with the musical aroma of my creation; all the sounds, all the characteristic motives are in my head so that, when the text is finished and the scenes are ordered, the actual opera is also completed, and the detailed musical treatment is more in the nature of a quiet and calm working-out process after the event, for the moment of real production is already past. But to this end one can choose only subjects which cannot be treated in any manner but a musical one: I would never choose a subject which, in the hands of a well-versed dramatist, could just as easily be turned into a spoken drama. But as a musician I can select subjects, I can invent situations and contrasts which must always remain a closed book to the dramatic author and to the spoken drama. This, in my opinion, is also the point where opera and drama come to a parting of the ways, and side by side both can calmly pursue their own aims.... For my next opera I have settled on the beautiful and strange Tannhäuser legend—Tannhäuser, who tarried in the Venus mountain and then made a penitential pilgrimage to Rome. I have merged this legend with the Minstrels' Contest on the Wartburg, where Tannhäuser takes the place of Heinrich von Ofterdingen. This fusion gives me a wealth of vitally dramatic content, and I believe the whole subject matter will make it apparent that it can only be fittingly handled by a musician.

This letter evinces a much clearer recognition of the basic facts than does the whole of his book *Oper und Drama*, and it also gives an exhaustive self-analysis of the poet-composer at work. One stipulation in this, however, must be seen in the right light, namely the notion of a telescopic perspective—that actually, once the text was completed, the work of the musician had already been done. This idea is correct as far as the basic creative invention is concerned, the original conception which contains the work as a whole as though in a germinal cell, just as the seed contains the whole tree with all its branches, twigs, leaves, blossoms and fruit. But the path which leads from the seed, from this germinal cell to the completed work is long and often thorny, and no step can be taken on this path without the blessings of inspiration and the inexplicable preparedness of imagination to do its job: out of the darkness, out of portent, out of groping feelings they have to produce something Promethean which, at any given moment, can fulfil the function which the work as an entity may demand. Complete organic unity is the great and inexplicable prerogative of a work of genius. It is a quality which communicates itself to the initiate just as immediately as he would distinguish between a real flower and an artificial one.

An unequivocal symptom of organic unity is the unmistakable individuality of every single one of Wagner's works from *Der fliegende Holländer* to *Parsifal*. For anyone reasonably acquainted with Wagner's works it is only necessary to hear a few bars of *Lohengrin, Tristan, Meistersinger* to know which opera they stem from, even if he may not immediately be able to place their exact occurrence within the drama. Each work has its own individual style. The phenomenon is not unique and can also be observed in the case of other great music dramatists such as Mozart and Verdi. In Wagner's case it bears an even more unambiguous stamp, probably caused by his more unusual and highly individualistic poetic and dramatic shaping of his text. Surprisingly enough this individual differentiation of style even applies to the four sections of the *Ring* tetralogy, despite their wealth of thematic interconnections—but here different causes come into play, of which more anon.

In the primary stages of the creative process when, so to speak, the material is still in a molten state, a composer may commit errors, both as far as the style and the quality of the invention is concerned. But a critically observant conscience will warn him in good time not to accept whatever is inadequate or stylistically alien. When Wagner was working on Act III of *Tristan* he wrote a letter to Mathilde Wesendonck which contains a most informative communication of this nature:

> Just imagine: recently, working on the gay shepherd's tune to accompany Isolde's crossing of the sea, suddenly another melodic phrase came to me which is much more jubilant, almost heroically jubilant, and yet it has a folk-like character. I was about to change everything round again when I finally realized that this tune does not belong to Tristan's shepherd, but to Siegfried! Immediately I looked up Siegfried's final verses with Brünnhilde and recognized that my melody fitted the words

> | *Sie ist mir ewig,* | "She is for ever, |
> |---|---|
> | *ist mir immer* | is for aye, |
> | *Erb und Eigen,* | my wealth and world, |
> | *Ein und All.* | my one and all." |
> | | (transl. Frederick Jameson) |

> It will sound incredibly daring and jubilant. But so, all of a sudden I was back in *Siegfried*. Should this not be enough to sustain my belief in my life and my—endurance?

And to illustrate the other case, inadequacy: in a letter to Mathilde from the time when he had just begun to compose *Meistersinger* he cites a melody intended for Walter von Stolzing:

Fern___ mei-ner Ju - gend gold - nen To - ren

zog___ ich einst aus,___ in Be-trach-tung ganz ver - lo - ren.

This philistine excrescence (and this applies to the words as well as to the music) Wagner fortunately rejected at a later stage and replaced it by the Prize Song, that precious gift of a blessed moment of inspiration. When it came to decisions such as this he was always guarded by the ever-watchful conscience of the mature artist and the categorical imperative of the work which would not tolerate any compromise. When, after sketching out Act II, he put *Siegfried* aside, this decision had external motivations, but nevertheless it is manifest that, as far as the *Ring* was concerned, the well of inspiration had dried up at the time. It seems that halfway through Act I of *Meistersinger* he had reached a similar *point mort* which may have been the cause of the restlessness and torment of those two years in Vienna and the subsequent years in Munich. Needless to say, in such cases it is impossible to decide which was cause and which effect. From Penzing he wrote to Mathilde on 28 June 1863:

> I am not yet a real master, and even in music I have not yet got far beyond the apprentice stage; God alone knows how it all will go! . . . Admit it, it is difficult for such a half-trained Mastersinger to write to you. If I were to say to you, for example, that a Master must have peace and quiet, then I would also have to admit at the same time that I have none and—that is the worst of it!—that I shall probably never have either. . . .

No matter; every discerning listener must gain the impression that in the convent of the assembly of the Masters in Act I the music gets bogged down, which is especially noticeable in contrast to the vitality of the preceding scene with the apprentices. With Pogner's address the music coalesces anew and regains its former intensity, and when Walter takes the stage this *point mort* is victoriously overcome. This indubitable crisis in the composition of *Meistersinger* may well be connected with the aridity of the scenic situation which had little to offer to the fantasy of the musician. Later more will be said about this problem in all music drama. Taken all in all, the composition of *Meistersinger* stood under a lucky star from the very beginning, in as much as it began with the terrific eruption of the Prelude, this first and immediate concept of the entire idea which, even before the text had been written, determined the style of the whole work completely and utterly and supplied an incomparable wealth of thematic material to boot. It was the only time that Wagner began with what normally was his finishing-up job. In general the overture is a sort of summary, the quintessence of the work—here it is the primordial concept from which the work itself grew, and every single bar of the Prelude eventually proved to be a thematic germ which fertilized the whole of the *Meistersinger* music.

It is not intended to analyse Wagner's works in detail, but there are certain factors of fundamental interest which must be discussed, which means that at least some characteristic aspects from among the wealth of material must be isolated and dissected. The beauty of the two Dresden works, *Tannhäuser* and *Lohengrin*, which were still created completely spontaneously, is the immediacy, uninfluenced by any kind of theory, with which the symbolic content of the fairy-tale action comes to life without the audience necessarily becoming aware of that content. In *Lohengrin* the essence of the tragedy is the impossibility of reconciling the Earthly with the Divine, for the Divine must always be a secret and vanishes when the veil of that secret is lifted. The same symbolism occurs in the fairy-tale of *Undine*, which has become another mainstay of romantic opera (E. T. A. Hoffmann, Lortzing, Kreutzer). In *Tannhäuser* it is the old struggle (which has its foundation in mediaeval asceticism) between profane and celestial love, between sin and repentance, and already in the Overture this is expressed in a musical symbolism of most impressive dimensions by the two principal motives, the Pilgrim's Chorus and the *Venusberg* Music. As in the *Holländer*, costumes, *décor*, the whole romantic façade vanish behind the genuine spontaneity of the musical utterance. Wagner truly must have experienced this contrition of a sinner with all his soul—and there can be no doubt that he must have lingered in the *Venusberg*. The orgiastic music which he heard from there is the most fascinating part of the *Tannhäuser* score: it is a sound of an intensity and luminosity such as only Wagner could conjure up. Yet there is much in this work which has become pallid, just because—much more so than *Der fliegende Holländer*—it is a transition to a new and not yet wholly mastered form of musical language. Wagner himself felt that the *Venusberg* scene in Act I was not up to standard, and hence the Paris revision which, however, did not do it much good either. Even worse are the weak sections in the scene of the Minstrels' Contest, because they are considerably longer. It is strange that just at the point where events should lead to a culmination of inspired singing the representation should get stuck in a meagre recitative in which a few aria-like episodes float around like scanty bits of meat in a watery broth. What obviously stunted the fantasy of the composer at this juncture was the sober didacticism with which "the essence of love" was to be debated at the drop of a hat. In the development of Wagner's music-dramatic concept this scene is of importance as the first attempt at a style which makes as its principal demand that every word should be clearly comprehensible. Unaccountably Wagner had a special predilection for this particular scene. The fact that it never came off does not seem to have taught him anything, for his irresistible urge towards verbosity remained unabated, since without it he simply could not imagine a dramatic motivation of the happenings. Whenever, listening to Wagner, our tension and our interest flag this is only due to one circumstance: the murderous thoroughness of his text which, with its descriptive, explanatory, long-winded content, paralysed the inspiration of the musician at its very roots.

In *Lohengrin* his new style has come to full maturity; it is now unified and almost free from relapses. This applies to Wagner's peculiar vocal articulation as well as to his orchestration which only now, after the experiences of all his earlier works, had gained that wonderful plasticity of design and tonal colouring in which no other composer had been able even to come near him. Here at long last he took a step for which the foundation had already been laid in Weber's *Euryanthe* and in Meyerbeer's *Les Huguenots* as well as in his own operas: the complete abolition of "numbers"—those recitatives, arias, duets and finales which traditionally formed the act of an opera and which had already been more and more frequently connected by transitions, doing away with those drastic endings which positively provoke applause. As in drama, the act now consists of various scenes which flow into each other without interruptions.

But this is only a superficiality. If one wanted to, one could easily divide up *Lohengrin* into "numbers" just like *Tannhäuser*. Quite naturally the music crystallizes into separate episodes because this corresponds to its very nature, and an organic tendency to such crystallization can also be found in all Wagner's works after *Lohengrin*. But this liberation from the conventional custom of individual "numbers" is an essential ingredient of his concept of a new operatic style and the pre-requisite for a structural manner which puts the aims of drama above those of music—in other words, he was no longer prepared to make concessions to the music which might have a negative influence on the structural demands of the drama. Even *Lohengrin* is already a masterly achievement in this respect. One has to turn to the greatest of all dramatists, to Shakespeare and Schiller, in order to find a dramatic build-up of similar tension to that in the first act of *Lohengrin* with its threefold, ever-increasing intensification which in the end leads to Lohengrin's victory in the duel and the exultant finale. Also in *Lohengrin* Wagner, at the age of thirty-five, created two pieces of music—the Preludes to Acts I and III—which he himself was never able to surpass as far as formal perfection, unique individuality of invention and splendour of orchestral colouring are concerned. At the same time they are diametrical opposites —the one an expression of tender transfiguration, the other of joyous and festive jubilation—and characterize the enormous span of Wagner's powers of imagination.

For *Lohengrin* he invented a new way of solving his problems (I at least do not know of any precedent in dramatic literature), one which he made use of again in *Tristan*. Up to then at best tragic heroines could escape into insanity, but it was so much simpler if they just died of grief. The brilliant Viennese author of farces, Nestroy, did not live to hear Isolde's love-death, but he wrote a *Lohengrin* parody, now long forgotten, which shows up his sharp, satirical powers of observation. In this parody Elsa dies with the words: "I don't need no dagger, I can die on me own." [This in broad—and untranslatable—Viennese dialect! HHS]

Wagner had no scruples whatsoever when it came to the means of realizing a dramatic concept. In this respect he had the same robust *insouciance* of all opera librettists, and more will have to be said about this later. There simply is no permanent equilibrium in the relationship between dramatist and composer: the one or the other occasionally has to make a sacrifice —and this is precisely what Wagner the Theorist would never have admitted. He himself probably never realized that he had made the original, decisive sacrifice long ago. At the time when, with full consciousness, he chose the path of music, he took with him the dramatist without whom he could not exist, without whom his brilliant musical inspiration could never have burst into full blossom; but it is an inescapable fact that it was the poet who got short shrift.

In reading a Wagner text without thinking of the music it is hardly possible to get through one single page without shuddering. There are no two ways about it: it simply must be accepted that Wagner just was not a poet—if by "poet" we mean someone who has an infallible instinct for verbal expression, for syllabic rhythm, for the unbelievable subtlety of the language mosaic of a line of verse—attributes which men such as (in German poetry) Goethe, Hölderlin, Mörike possessed in the highest degree. Of these attributes Wagner apparently had not the faintest notion. He did not need those qualities because he replaced them by a melodic vocal line which, guided by the accents of the words, speaks its own language. His talent simply developed in a different direction, and this development obviously could not take place without an atrophy of poetry *per se*. The poet had to sacrifice himself for the musical dramatist, and the expressive beauty, the innermost soul of poetic words had to fall by the wayside.

The doorway of Wagner's Bayreuth villa is graced by the following words:

> *Hier, wo mein Wähnen Frieden fand,*
> *WAHNFRIED*
> *sei dieses Haus von mir benannt.*

("Here, where my quest was pacified, Wahnfried let me name this house".)

Anyone who writes "poetry" of this order must put up with the fact that the wags nickname him the *Wahnfriedrich* [Untranslatable! HHS]. It is even less surprising that the continual alliteration of the *Ring* text and particularly such ejaculations as *Weia, waga* or *Hojotoho, heiaha* could not help provoking satirical treatment. During the *Rheingold* rehearsals in Munich there were some difficulties with the three Rhine Maidens because of the breakneck convolutions which they had to execute on swings invisible to the audience. At that time the Munich equivalent of *Punch* came out with a little quatrain which may perhaps be rendered as:

> Wigala, wogala wick,
> If I stay on the swing I'll be sick;
> Wigala, wogala weck,
> If I fall I'll break me neck.

In *Tristan* the romantically emotional paroxysms lead to the most extravagant hypertrophy of lyrical metaphor. Page after page one stumbles over passages of which a real poet would never have been guilty, such as the following lines:

> *Was wir dachten, was uns däuchte,*
> *all Gedenken, all Gemahnen,*
> *heil' ger Dämm'rung hehres Ahnen*
> *löscht des Wähnens Graus*
> *welterlösend aus.*

"What we thought, what we sensed,
all recollection, all reminiscence,
the holy dawn of sublime vision
are effaced in the horrifying purge
of universal salvation."

This pompous balderdash is completely submerged, dissolved, transmuted in the music. It offered singable words to the composer, and apparently that was all he needed for his purpose at that moment. His music took care of the poetic utterance, and his lyricism was in no way fettered by such verbal spaghetti. It is worse when the spate of words becomes descriptive, reflective, philosophical, as is the case in the great love scene in the first half of Act II, where the conflict between day and night is discussed interminably:

Doch es rächte sich der verscheuchte Tag,
mit deinen Sünden Rats er pflag:
was dir gezeigt die dämmernde Nacht,
an des Tagesgestirnes Königsmacht
musstest du's übergeben,
um einsam in öder Pracht
schimmernd dort zu leben.

"But vengeance took the frightened day,
which had counsel with your sins:
what dusky night had shown you,
to the regal might of the day star
you had to surrender it,
and alone, in solitary splendour,
shimmeringly, you must live there."

To get over this hurdle may have caused the composer some difficulties—at least that is the impression one gets. In this scene the best way out is a well-devised cut although, with Wagner's complicated, interweaving method of composition, cuts are never a simple matter. Strangely enough, despite his great touchiness as far as cuts were concerned, Wagner was never unconditionally against them. Especially in *Tristan*, where he was very well aware of the immense physical exertion to which he was subjecting his protagonists, he was quite amenable to cuts, particularly in Act III. To Ludwig Schnorr, his first Tristan, he wrote:

> It is quite thinkable and even possible that one day this third act of *Tristan* may be performed completely without omissions, but in the first performances this cannot possibly happen. If such an exuberant throw is to succeed at all, it can only be under exceptionally happy conditions for which not even the most talented person can predestine a given day. For that reason it would be my advice not to perform this act in its entirety at once, not under any circumstances, even if the singers could do it immediately, because it would be more than daring to present the theatre audience at the very first performances with such a breadth of dramatic vision.

And to another of his heroic tenors, Albert Niemann: "I really should go through *Tristan* again and 'humanize' him for theatre evenings, etc.; all I need is a little spare time. As things stand it is asking too much, for in every respect that is asking for the impossible."

Questions of practical performance can never be dealt with summarily, for during the course of a century the attitude to this problem has completed a full circle. For decades uncut performances of Wagner's works have been possible because of the fascination of his music, because one did not feel any tedious lengths or at least was unwilling to be upset by them. Nowadays things are different; the practical exigencies of the theatre have to be accepted (in some cases this has already been realized) and in the interest of the overall effectiveness of Wagner's music the problem of cuts must be dealt with—but as discreetly and musically as possible.

4

THE PHANTOM OF THE
GESAMTKUNSTWERK

... From assemblies of state, from the law courts, from the countryside and from the ships, from military camps and from the most remote regions, the nation gathers and fills the amphitheatre in their thirty-thousands to see a production of that most deeply moving of all tragedies, *Prometheus* [by Aeschylus], to become a collective entity before this mightiest of all works of art, to comprehend its own *raison d'être*, to fuse into a unity of its own entelechy, its oneness, and with its God so that, in an ideal calm, it could merge again as that which, a few hours ago, in hurried agitation and separate individuality, it had equally been. . . . In tragedy the people of Greece found its innermost self, that noblest part of its being, united with the noblest aspects of the entity of an entire nation. . . .

THIS IS THE way in which Wagner, in his treatise *Die Kunst und die Revolution* ("Art and Revolution"), explained the relationship between art and life in ancient Greece, in the golden age of a state based on an idealistic social order. The fact that this state could not have existed without slave labour did not bother him in the least—but, of course, his reflections had the advantage of being based on fantasies anyway. Wagner's fellow-revolutionaries in Dresden may well often have despaired of him as a visionary who could not differentiate between fact and wishful thinking. When he was in exile he tried to systematize his ideas, and Greek theatre, which his study of the classic tragedians and Platonic philosophy had brought close to him, formed the hub of all his considerations. Now he found a nexus with his actual situation. The dualism of his collision with the political system on the one hand, and his artistic conflict with operatic tradition on the other, turned his speculations in the direction of a concatenation of all those facts, deficiencies and obstacles which were undesirable to him. Out of all this arose his concept of an ideal state in which the artist was to play the only part which could possibly suffice for him: to be the spiritual centre as a seer and prophet.

In the history of music the humanistic vision of Greek drama has always exerted a profound influence on opera, from the very first musico-dramatic experiments of the Renaissance onwards. But it remained a mirage with Monteverdi as it did with Gluck and Wagner, for what we know of Greek drama is restricted to the poetry; of the music we have practically no knowledge, and so it is impossible to form a picture of the overall effect. The nobility of the modest number of dramatic masterpieces of Greek art, literature and philosophy which escaped the destruction of documents during the early Christian period justifies the interest in this world of the past which has never flagged since the days of the Renaissance. But this lost world cannot be reconstructed, and its sociological, artistic and religious precepts cannot be transferred to a completely differently organized civilization. Wagner's entire edifice is nothing but an illusion.

The French philosopher and aesthete Henri Lichtenberger wrote a tome entitled *Richard Wagner, Poète et Penseur* ("R.W., Poet and Thinker"). This was also Wagner's own opinion of himself, and as such the congregation of faithful Wagnerians and later the whole world adulated him. He was neither. The poet we have already discussed; to be a thinker, despite his intellectual powers of penetration and his broad outlook, he lacked one fundamental characteristic without which objective thought is impossible: he was incapable of searching his own conscience. Instead he rationalized his day-dreams, and hence the unbounded subjectivity of his conclusions. The existing social order was no good because he, Wagner, had collided with it. And as the art of the theatre such as it happened to be did not grant him the possibility of standing clearly perceivable on the highest pinnacle, it was utterly to be damned and had to make way for a new and better form of art—and the achievement of this object was, of course, his personal task. He was the

only one who could dare perform the synthesis of all existing
means of art and thereby realize that ideal which had never been
reached again since the days of ancient Greece: the *Kunstwerk
der Zukunft*, the *Gesamtkunstwerk*.

To this end he first had to counter the supposition that there
was such a thing as "modern art". As far as opera was concerned the proof was easy: opera had weaknesses which could be
attacked from the aesthetic point of view and which were
difficult to defend. But how about instrumental music, how
about Beethoven whom Wagner himself idolized? Here again
the Ninth had to come to the rescue:

> Beethoven's last symphony is the salvation of music from out
> of its very own element into an all-embracing form of art. It
> is the human gospel of the Art of the Future. No further
> progress is possible, for it can only have one direct successor:
> the perfect art work of the future, the all-embracing drama,
> for which Beethoven himself has forged the artistic key. . . .
> For his contemporary and later composers those forms in
> which the Master proclaimed his artistic, historic struggle
> just remained forms. They became mannerisms, a matter of
> fashion, and although no instrumental composer had any-
> thing worthwhile left to say in those forms yet none of them
> despaired, and they continued to write symphonies and
> similar works without ever hitting on the idea that actually
> the last symphony had already been written. (From *Das
> Kunstwerk der Zukunft*.)

And so Schubert, Mendelssohn, Schumann have been successfully disposed of, not to mention many a minor composer. And
as for drama? Here Wagner proves that even the German
classics were already in rather a sorry state:

> Even Schiller's dramatic creations we can see caught between
> two poles: a wavering between history and fiction on the one
> hand, the perfect form of Greek drama on the other. . . . So
> Schiller remained suspended in mid-air between heaven and
> earth. . . . The most recent dramatic poetry which, as a form of
> art, only lives on the literary monuments of Goethe's and

Schiller's attempts, has continued this wavering between the two opposing directions mentioned above to the point of tottering.

And the theatre as an artistic institution?

Generally speaking our theatrical institutions have no other purpose than to furnish an entertainment which is repeated evening after evening, which is not vitally demanded, but which is dominated by a spirit of speculation and accepted casually by the social boredom of the populace of our cities.

Vis-à-vis all these deficiencies we have the idealistic postulate:

An artistic person can only be fully satisfied by the union of all forms of art in one combined work. If his artistic capabilities are dismembered he is unfree, not completely what he could be, whereas in the combined work of art he is free and completely what he can be. . . . The highest form of a combined work of art is drama, and it can only exist in its greatest possible fullness if every form of art is represented in it with such fullness.

It is superfluous to go further into the matter. None of the above conclusions and claims can withstand even the most casual examination. Wagner's concept is based on a convenient neglect of all the presuppositions of development in new music and literature, quite apart from the absurdity of behaving as though, in his Ninth Symphony, Beethoven had created something completely novel by combining instruments and voices, and as though afterwards he had not composed the greatest and loftiest which it is possible to imagine in instrumental music when he wrote his last five string quartets—works which Wagner loved above all. But all this is irrelevant compared with the fact that these theories were of vital necessity to Wagner because they strengthened him in the unshakeable belief in his mission, that belief which moves mountains. But the great danger is that a doctrine which is absurd in its very nature must also lead to absurd results unless the instinct of the artist is stronger than

F

all theory. The towering greatness of Wagner's mature works is only thanks to the circumstance that, when it came to the point, he was quite prepared to forget about his doctrines. But then he never was pedantic in the matter of his principles. His rabid anti-semitism in no way prevented him from being close friends with Carl Tausig, Heinrich Porges, Hermann Levi, Josef Rubinstein and Angelo Neumann, all of them Jewish. He was a confirmed vegetarian and loved beefsteak. His condemnation of all instrumental music neither prevented him from writing and publishing Album Leaves and the *Siegfried-Idyll*, nor from highly recommending two piano quintets of the Italian composer Giovanni Sgambati to his publisher Schott—the latter with a nasty dig at the "tedious chamber music" of Brahms—and during the last years of his life he was planning to compose some "cheerful symphonies" which, unfortunately, he did not live long enough to write.

Despite it all the chimera of Greek theatre never ceased to occupy his thoughts. This is most evident in the monumental conception of *Der Ring des Nibelungen*, which at that time was dominating his imagination and which may well have had a decisive influence on his artistic philosophy. On the other hand, ignoring all practical considerations, he would hardly have planned such an extravagant *magnum opus* if no theory of such vast and intoxicating import had captivated his mind and convinced him of the justification, nay, the necessity of so grandiose a creation. Greece had its trilogies drawn from its great myths—the tragedies of the House of the Atreidai, and of Oedipus. Now Wagner placed the Nibelungen saga side by side with those classical masterpieces as being their peer from amongst the German cycles of legends and declared that mythology is the only worthy subject-matter of drama because mythology alone, by reason of its general humanism and its deeply symbolical background, could affect the emotions of an audience with real directness. From Old High German and Nordic sources he adopted alliteration, which he thus declared to be the most suitable form of versification for music drama. Fortunately he abandoned that hobby-horse when it came to the works following the *Ring—Tristan und Isolde, Die Meistersinger, Parsifal.* As far as the *Ring* is concerned, he initially adhered to the fundamental principle of Greek theatre: the idea that performance of such an extraordinary work must not be left to everyday theatrical life, but must be a festival, a unique national and artistic event of outstanding splendour which would unite the nation as a cultural community, just as it once had done in the Greece of antiquity. Over and over he stressed that next to his artistic aims he had the great national goal to create a new form of art which, born entirely out of the German spirit, would express the essence of everything German in the most characteristic manner. After the last *Ring* performance in Bayreuth he addressed the audience and said: "You have seen what can be done. Now it is up to you to will it. And if you do so will it, we shall have true art." The firm conviction that he was the first and only one to make come true the German artistic ideal—despite Schiller and Goethe, Bach, Mozart, Beethoven and Schubert—never left him for a moment. Out of this conviction he wrote to the Schnorrs after the Munich performance of *Tristan*:

The incomparable has been done. And if really one day this most peculiar German art should bear the fruit which I can visualize in my mind, the depth and beauty of which must surpass everything which any nation has ever created to its glory, then be assured that you, my friends, will never be forgotten on earth, for your feat was the source of the spring which gave warmth to my work, strength and light to my urge!

There were men who achieved great things, but probably never another like Wagner, who needed such colossal illusions to achieve them.

There are two possible reasons for such an over-estimation of oneself: either one has a higher opinion of one's own work than corresponds to the facts, or one underestimates the work of others. In Wagner's case it is in the main the latter tendency, a tendency in which he is pretty well unique amongst the famous musicians of his century. This great personality suffered from restrictions of his artistic horizon such as are, as a rule, only encountered in amateurs. His creative output as well as his immediate relationship to music—be it as listener or as inter-preter—were almost entirely concentrated on primary emotions. He never took any notice of the opposite aspect of music, that joy of music-making which is fostered by objective impulses and the sheer delight in polyphony, rhythms and forms: for him all this represented nothing but a history of the past which had to be overcome. The rare exceptions of such impulsive music-making which can be found in Wagner only prove the rule, because they can be explained directly *by* the rules. He had to think of a gay shepherd's tune in *Tristan*, something completely objective which only accompanies the action from outside, in order to find a jubilant motive for his Siegfried (cf. p. 149):

Similarly he needed the imaginative vision of the archaically pedantic, self-confident guilds of Nürnberg to conjure up the grandiose phenomenon of the *Meistersinger* Prelude, and with it the incomparably pictorial contrast between a world which rests firmly on an objective concept of form, and the world of Walter von Stolzing with its exuberant expressiveness and its inspired emotions. The objective, *classical* world was a closed book to him unless he could identify it with a costume, just as he himself had to have a costume in order to reach that state of trance-like concentration which he needed—his silk shirts and underwear, his precious dressing-gowns, his velvet berets, and with them the soft, rich colours of his curtains and furniture coverings as well as an incredible array of scent- and perfume-bottles. It would be most tempting to investigate how much of romanticism could be considered a symptom running parallel with the flamboyance of a Makart.

Wagner's exclusive preoccupation with primary emotion in music even applies to the one and only of the "Great" before whom he bent his knee, to Beethoven, whose classical aspect, his cool, objective form-consciousness, lay outside everything which, to Wagner was, of interest in the music. To all the other classics he stood in a relationship of historical distance, at best with condescending acknowledgment that even those old fogies had managed to achieve something. Although he had grown up in Leipzig he knew little more of Bach than "The Well-Tempered Clavier", and when he played some Bach in Bayreuth it was usually one of the lyrical, emotive preludes which were his special favourites. When in Wahnfried a quartet played for him Beethoven's C major (the third of the Rasumovsky Quartets) he virtually discarded it out of hand as belonging to the "Sonata-Beethoven" in whom he was not interested. Nor did he enjoy Beethoven's Fourth Symphony, and when it came to *Fidelio* he could find nothing but weaknesses and dramatic deficiencies in it. A musician of his calibre could hardly by-pass Mozart without raising his hat, but his admiration for *Die Zauberflöte* and *Don Giovanni* was tempered by the fact that in them he mainly saw all the conventionalities of form and expression (and he would probably not have heard more than the "Sonata-Mozart" in a work such as the *Jupiter* Symphony). Händel he ignored. Haydn's "Creation" gave him some pleasure when he first met up with it in Dresden, where he conducted a performance of it, and he first heard "The Seasons" in Paris in 1858. At that time he was somewhat amused by the enjoyment of the audience "who regarded the regular cadential melismata at the conclusion of musical phrases, which are completely strange to modern music but so super-abundant in Haydn, as particularly original and charming traits". Many a song of Schubert's he valued—*Sei mir gegrüsst, Ständchen*—but he could and would not understand what his friend Liszt could see in the "bourgeois stolidity" of Schubert's trios and sonatas. To find a similarly narrow-minded taste we have to turn to one of Wagner's most hostile opponents, to Hanslick, for whom music only existed as a reality when, so to speak, he could grasp it with his hands as a melodically determined "moving pattern of sound". This last is Hanslick's own formulation—and Bach's music to him was as antiquated as it was to Wagner.

Dispassionate conviction about the progressive principle in music, and lack of respect for the masterworks of the past, form an essential part of the defensive mechanism of Wagner's self-esteem. Neither the past nor the present were allowed to stand in his way, and if anyone had ever dared tell him that the despised composer of *Il Trovatore* could one day create a music drama of masterly proportions he would have either argued his opponent to death—or himself. But if he had recognized the incomprehensible, incomparable heights of Mozart's great operas and Beethoven's *Fidelio* he would have been incapable of pursuing a diametrically opposed ideal of musico-dramatic form such as he had evolved in *Oper und Drama*. To forsake that phantom would have been artistic suicide for him.

The most realistic facet of this phantom is his superiority as a dramatist in comparison to the run-of-the-mill opera librettist. When it comes to the music, matters are not so simple, hence Wagner's endless attempts in *Oper und Drama* to prove all other operatic forms, present and past, invalid. His main argument is that drama cannot suffer the arrogance of the musicians claiming that individual pieces of music could be inserted although they bring the action to a standstill, or even that music could be the more important partner in this union. (Mozart, however, wrote: "In an opera poetry simply has to be the obedient daughter of music.") The obvious counter-question is to ask how the music is to be shaped, if it is not allowed to develop according to its own formal principles. Wagner has a brilliant answer to this question. As the vocal line is no longer coerced into the strait-jacket of the aria form, it will follow the declamation of the words with expressive faithfulness and leave the actual shaping of the form (without which music certainly cannot exist) to the sovereignty of the orchestra which now, liberated from the pettiness of the old "number" principle, can accompany the stage-action with the "infinite melody" of a great symphonic movement. The orchestra has the same role as the chorus in Greek drama: it accompanies the events as an eloquent commentator who reflects every detail, and whose decisiveness of expression originates in the fact that the thematic materials of this symphony, its themes and motives, have a poetic and thereby dramatico-psychological import. In this context Wagner uses the term *Erinnerungsmotiv*, "motif of reminiscence" (the Wagner commentators Porges and Wolzogen later invented the term *Leitmotiv*, "leading motif", but Wagner himself never used that expression), which before him Weber had used in his operas and Berlioz in his poetically-programmatically designed symphony. In Wagner's earlier works—*Holländer*, *Tannhäuser*, *Lohengrin*—this *Erinnerungsmotiv* already played an important part, but it still lived a separate life from the individually constructed "number", the aria or the duet, and was merely a link, an association of ideas to stimulate the imagination of the listener. When, in the Minstrels' Contest, Tannhäuser begins his last verse, which is to cause his own undoing, we hear a characteristic motif from the *Venusberg* music which indicates the train of his thoughts. In the same way, and with intense sympathy, we realize Elsa's torment when the orchestra ominously propounds the theme of Lohengrin's *Nie sollst du mich befragen* ("This question never ask me"). In both cases the effect is immediate, because the inner meaning is as immediate as the plasticity of the musical appearance. Things become more complicated—and we get involved in a maze of criss-cross connections—when the whole of the music consists of nothing but such allusions and innuendoes which sometimes appear contrapuntally on top of each other, sometimes in fragmentary fashion, such as is often the case in the *Ring*. In the early years of this century, when the Wagner cult was at its apex, there were librettos with inserted sheets on which all the "motifs" were listed and numbered. Numbers in the text itself pointed to the corresponding motif, and it was the sacred duty of the intelligent listener to follow the musical happenings along those lines. This nonsense, thank goodness, is now over and done with. It only confirms what a little critical thought should have made obvious from the very start: that the presupposition is purely theoretical, because the intended association of ideas will not come about under bombardment. The *Erinnerungsmotiv*, which can be of the deepest meaning in musical drama, loses its effect completely when it becomes a mannerism and occurs *ad nauseam*.

Forgetting for the moment about beautiful exceptions in the *Ring*, in *Tristan* and in *Meistersinger*, this mosaic of *Erinnerungs-motive* has nothing to do with symphonic structure. In a symphonic development the entry of themes and motives is determined by musical reasons, by the pregnancy and contrast of those ideas and by the vast planes of a construction which is designed to bring everything into a unity. By the rules of the *Leitmotiv* principle the motif does not appear because the form of the music demands it, but simply because the apposite cue has turned up in the text. If the text does not promote a lyrical or dramatic expression, this only results in an arid quotation, devoid of any musical connotation or necessity, and such a sequence of quotations must lack the essence of symphonic structure: a continuous line. Like the *Gesamtkunstwerk* as such, the "orchestra symphony" shaped merely out of symbolic motifs is a phantasmagoria.

The greatness of Wagner's artistic achievement is due to the fact that he had an innate ability to avoid the traps which he had set for himself. Most conspicuous in this respect is the *Meistersinger* Prelude, where all his thematic invention flows as an immediate and logical consequence from his inspiration, and the various motifs—if one may say so—only realize their symbolic character at a later stage. There are also cases such as the Prelude to Act II of *Meistersinger*, the Ride of the Valkyries and the Magic Fire Music in *Walküre* where the creative fantasy of the composer took command of those tone-symbols and, inspired by a strong dramatic vision, developed them in an organic manner. Granted, this is a *sine qua non* of symphonic procedure, but no more than that. Even when Wagner comes close to the superficial impression of a symphonist, as in the *Meistersinger* Prelude, he still remains an opera composer. His means may be more opulent, his instrumentation and technique more brilliant, yet he follows, as he did in the Overtures to *Der fliegende Holländer* and *Tannhäuser*, the Weber model of a conglomerate of episodes put together with paste and scissors which only has a very superficial resemblance to the formal structure of the first movement of a symphony. The truth of the matter can be seen in those passages which are not real transitions, but more or less "gummings-together". In the *Holländer* Overture— which nevertheless is a splendid and inspired work—they are even more obviously, embarrassingly primitive. One need only look at the transition to the coda (in D major, 2/2) which introduces the final apotheosis with an *arpeggio* on a diminished seventh chord, spread out in a manner which can be found in any elementary piano tutor or collection of exercises:

Passages of such naïveté can no longer be found in the *Tannhäuser* Overture. What we find there is a sturdy operatic melody, Tannhäuser's hymn to Venus, a blatantly unsymphonic element which could come straight from one of Weber's opera overtures. In his next work, *Lohengrin*, Wagner abandoned the overture in favour of a terse Prelude moulded from a single thematic complex, and instinctively made the best possible decision. Here, as in the *Tristan* Prelude, he achieved the greatest height of symphonic composition of which he was capable. In a composition of real thematic consistency his scope was limited by the expansive capacities of a single main idea—which incorporates the essence of the entire work— and its derivatives. In the *Meistersinger* Prelude he returned once more to the form of Weber's overtures, but now he handled that form with masterly sovereignty. But this still does not make it symphonic in the true sense of the word.*

* Alfred Lorenz, *Das Geheimnis der Form bei Richard Wagner* ("The Secret of R. W.'s Form") (1924) is an attempt in several volumes to discover that secret. As it excited some comment at the time it may be just as well to point out that there is no secret as such. Of course, one can prove lots of things with graphs and diagrams, but in the same way one can also prove the contrary. Wagner would have been highly amused had he seen Lorenz's constructions. When Lorenz goes into details he only finds what every intelligent listener will discern in any case: that each of the many episodes which make up a Wagnerian operatic act, corresponding to his intuitive sense of form, has become an organically constructed musical miniature. What *is* essential is that they remain episodes and never become a formal structure which encompasses the whole act, as this would also contradict all dramatic sense. It is symptomatic that in the one case where Wagner really strove for the great and all-embracing form, namely in the *Meistersinger* Prelude, Lorenz has misunderstood it completely: he has overlooked that

No artist evolves a technique which is not essential to him. Wagner's sense of form is completely directed towards the stage, wholly born out of the right instinct that operatic effects will always be a sequence of episodic effects. Whatever music he invents is therefore invariably of an episodic nature and consequently in antithesis to symphonic characteristics. Glorious conceptions such as the Ride of the Valkyries, the Magic Fire Music, the Forest Murmurs, Siegfried's Journey down the Rhine stand up very well without any major formal structure: the idea as such and the flood of invention which it pours forth is sufficient unto itself. Once the flow of invention has dried up, the piece is over or, as in the case of the *Meistersinger* Prelude, it is followed immediately by a new idea which expands into another episode with the same self-sufficiency. In the last-named work the contrapuntal combination of three main motives—in the sense of symphonic form it is a shortening of the recapitulation by telescoping the themes—is effective in an operatically-superficial manner, but as a compositional achievement it is of dubious distinction: the great contrapuntalist Wagner has done better elsewhere.

As a symphonist he utterly lacked concern, and this is one of the sources of his irresistible magic. In his criticism of the first Wagner concert in Vienna in 1862 Hanslick spoke of the *demagogic* effect of Wagner's music, an expression which is not at all badly chosen. Just as the demagogue makes his effect by an inciting slogan, so Wagner makes his by an invention as powerful as elementary nature. Apparently the critic had sensed the genius behind the conception and then rationalized his rejection of the entire phenomenon Wagner (with which he was out of sympathy) by the argument that it was unfair to achieve effects by such means.

There were moments when Wagner more or less became aware of the non-symphonic character of his music. In an article *Über die Anwendung der Musik auf das Drama* ("The Use

---

Walter's love-song in E (which later becomes the *Abgesang*, the epilogue, of the Prize Song) is the second subject of a clearly laid out sonata form, and that the parodistic diminution (E flat) of the Mastersingers' theme introduces the development section. No—as far as his work is concerned Wagner never kept a secret to himself!

of Music in Drama") written for the *Bayreuther Blätter* he raised
this point, and his argument turned clearly against Bruckner
who adulated him with child-like devotion: "In its proper
sense a principal subject of a symphonic movement whose
harmonies modulate so noticeably is unthinkable, especially if
from its very first appearance it presents itself in such a
bewildering guise." Then he quotes Elsa's entry in Act I of
Lohengrin as an example that, although anything of that kind
would be impermissible in a symphony, it was decidedly in its
right place in opera:

What he said here applies equally to the Pilgrims' Chorus
and the *Venusberg* Music in the *Tannhäuser* Overture as well as
to all his most fascinating creations—precisely those which
Hanslick termed demagogic, for the Ride of the Valkyries and
the Magic Fire Music which were played in that concert are
definitely of that type. They are orchestral conceptions of
inimitable luminosity and plasticity resulting from the finest
craftsmanship and a detailed working-out of the harmonic
plan. For the connoisseur a Wagner score is a picture book of
incomparable charm, and it should be noted that in the Ride
of the Valkyries a baroque Venetian technique—a grouping
together of various instruments into choruses such as can be
found in the opening movement of Bach's *Magnificat* or in the
Sanctus of his B minor Mass—had reached an unprecedented
height of virtuosity. Three independent tonal planes are

superimposed—the trills of the woodwind, the descending
arpeggios of the strings, the dotted riding rhythm of bassoons
and horns—and against this background the bass trumpet
reinforced by two horns propounds the Valkyries motif so that
it really appears like the riding Valkyries against a background
of storm-tossed clouds.

For reasons stated above there is nothing symphonic about
all this. And as Wagner's claim to the laurels of a symphonist is
untenable it is obviously necessary to investigate his other
claim, that of being a dramatist of the highest order. In this
investigation it would not be fair to go back to his early works,
which admittedly are operas pure and simple. But those early
works give an indication of the original direction of his dramatic
concept. For that reason they are not without importance, and
if then one submits Wagner's later music dramas to a critical
examination, if one takes into consideration certain corresponding characteristics which are to be found everywhere, and if one
thinks of the surroundings in which Wagner grew up, then the
background of his dramatic ideas emerges as an unambiguous
fact: romantic melodrama.

This expression was coined because it characterizes the
peculiarities of opera in the romantic era in a typical way. It is
here that the romantic trend towards all that is fantastic and
emotional found its most fertile soil and its most enthusiastic
public. The ageing Goethe, whose judgment was deeply rooted
in classic calm and simplicity of action, recognized the merits
of the *Freischütz* libretto with kindness and gave it the stamp
of his approval. This could only be because to him it was
completely natural that in opera such a plump, fantastic text
should be raised by music on to another plane, far removed
from all earthly reality, and this he considered apt and fitting.
Romantic opera drew many subjects from contemporary
literature, above all from Walter Scott and Victor Hugo. But
the phenomenon as such dates back further; it can already be
found in Schiller's *Die Räuber*, in Grillparzer's *Ahnfrau*. The most
unconcerned attitude to melodramatics, however, belongs
without doubt to Wagner's epoch: Donizetti's *Lucia di
Lammermoor* (Walter Scott), Verdi's *Ernani* and *Rigoletto*
(Victor Hugo) are typical examples of a dramatic trend which

is unbounded when it comes to blood and thunder, to exaggerated emotions laid on with a thick brush, where innocence is as white as the driven snow and evil tarred with the pitch of hell. Meyerbeer's *grand opéra* had combined this sort of dramatics with great historic subjects and the corresponding ostentation.

It would be quite understandable if an artist as ingenious and critically aware as Wagner had turned away unconditionally from such a trend, but he remained a child of his time. His criticism was directed against the formal principles, not against the contents of the romantic drama, because at bottom it was the soil in which he himself had his roots. He clearly recognized the barbaric nonsense as such of Weber's *Euryanthe*, but this did not stop him from taking that pair of intriguers, Eglantine and Lysiart, to his bosom and adapting them for his *Lohengrin*, just as he borrowed the duel as a divine judgment concerning the innocence of the heroine from Marschner's *Der Templer und die Jüdin* (based on Walter Scott's *Ivanhoe*). There is nothing to be said against this, for dramatic subjects have a habit of recurring. But they are typically melodramatic motives, and Ortrud is just as repulsive a witch as is Weber's Eglantine, even though Wagner has done his best to give her a background and demoniac proportions by making her a fanatical adherent of the unseated Nordic Gods. When it comes to motivation his invention is inexhaustible, but unfortunately at times also of catastrophic fussiness.

In life Wagner's urge for talking and arguing must have gone beyond all bounds, bordering on a vice. On one occasion he apparently overdid it to such an extent that even *he* felt compelled to apologize to Mathilde Wesendonck after the event—it was when Gottfried Semper had attacked "bestial seriousness":

But the moment I had uttered my words I cooled down, and I was only aware of a necessity—this I felt within myself—to lead the conversation back into more conventional channels. At the same time I was guided by an inner conviction that this could not be done by suddenly lapsing into silence, but only by a gradual, conscious and intelligible transition. I well remember that, even when I was still speaking forcibly, voicing my opinions, I thought I was conducting the conversation with a certain artistic intention, bringing it to a conclusion with understanding and in a placatory manner.... You yourself, I believe, became perturbed on that evening and feared that my continued, initially still forceful manner of speaking was due to my lasting excitement; and yet I remember also that I replied to you very calmly: "Please, do let me get back to the subject—that cannot be done so swiftly!"

Despite his unparalleled instinct for stage effects Wagner ever becomes the victim of his indomitable urge for argumentation, and there are moments when it is impossible to suppress the opposite feeling: must it really all be so involved? But it is just as with his aesthetic theories: when he is unsure of himself his verbal voluminosity knows no bounds. He is a melodramatist with a bad conscience, but on the other hand he cannot free himself from melodrama, much though he tries to turn it into true drama by a greater absorption in his individual characters and by complicated explanations.

One of the typical standard prerequisites of melodrama has already been touched upon: the intriguer. Wagner's intriguers and antagonists present a sorry spectacle because the music that goes with them is so poverty-stricken: obviously Wagner had no great affection for them. The music which he composed for them is rarely more than a sonorous backdrop. It clearly shows that he rejected them, which is not surprising. As an example one only has to look at Verdi to see what an overt, unashamed melodramatist could do with such antagonists, from Sparafucile (*Rigoletto*), Count di Luna (*Trovatore*), Carlos (*Forza del Destino*), Renato (*Ballo in Maschera*), Amonasro (*Aida*) right up to the incomparable Iago in *Otello*. What down-to-earth reality, what super-abundance of music! Wagner's intriguers are insufferably glum. Telramund is sadly henpecked, Hunding is an uncouth boor (the only things he has to say to his wife concern food and bed), Hagen is grim (Gunter calls him a churl), Klingsor has unsexed himself, and Alberich just plain curses.

All this cursing! The magic of the curse is another one of those melodramatic props which was invented at that time. The Old Testament knew the magic of blessing, but the curse was the prerogative of the Almighty and he hardly ever made use of it, possibly only against Cain. This melodramatic curse we find in Verdi—in *Rigoletto*, in *Forza del Destino*—and there it has its rightful and proper place. In Wagner it becomes a dramatic stop-gap against which much can be said. Alberich at least curses in order to safeguard his own immediate interests: first he curses love in order to get the gold, and then he curses the gold in order to defeat the robbers' ends. But Kundry curses without rhyme or reason simply because she is irritated, and it is difficult to understand why such a curse should be so effective as to send that poor, innocent Parsifal roaming the wilderness for years and years. Alberich can base his curse on a symbol, hence the curse of the gold is comprehensible. With Kundry no such symbol can be discerned. But some sort of symbol must be an *ad hoc* explanation, especially when it comes to another melodramatic remedy, namely the magic potion. It is quite possible that Wagner had his first inspiration for this magic potion, Queen Isolde included, from that comic opera *L'Elisir d'amore* by the despised Donizetti which was so popular at the time. At a pinch it is possible, in *Tristan*, to accept this love potion as a symbol of an irresistible attraction between two young people, even though the fatal mix-up with the death potion would make the whole action *quasi*-comic if it were not for the tragic background. Was it really so impossible for that nitwit Brangäne to find a more salubrious nostrum in Isolde's medicine chest when she was commanded to prepare the death potion?

And when we come to *Götterdämmerung* and the potion which turns Siegfried into a hare-brained marionette who no longer has the foggiest notion of what he is doing, the dramatic necessity can no longer be justified by any manner or means: it is just one of the clearly obvious deficiencies of *Götterdämmerung* in which the whole incongruency of the mythological motives of the *Nibelungen* cycle becomes so apparent. Everything goes in different directions, and what does not *belong* together has to be *forced* together willy-nilly. Whether we like it or not, the

Siegfried who killed the dragon, the husband of Gutrune (originally Krimhilde), and the Sigurd who awakened Brünnhilde and made her his wife were two different personages in the story and so, by means of a little potion, they have to be turned into one. On top of it all there is this strange, treacherous involvement with the principal prop, the ring: first Siegfried has given it to Brünnhilde, now he pulls it off her finger (do heroes always do that when they wrestle with women?), but the next morning he is completely oblivious of his heroic deed, whereas he can remember quite clearly that he had won this ring from the dragon Fafner. The potion apparently was highly selective: forgetfulness or non-forgetfulness, depending on the demands of the dramatic situation.

But if one gets to the bottom of the events of the *Ring*, there is no end to the absurdities. Just think: Wotan, this weird, irrational so-called God, has a palace built for himself. He does not possess the necessary means, and so he pawns his sister-in-law Freia, who, for pure reasons of survival (the golden apples!), is indispensable to the Gods; so most unwillingly he redeems her with gold which, in any case, he has stolen. It is impossible not to draw a parallel between this and Wagner himself, who was brilliant at borrowing money and equally loath to repay his debts, just as one cannot help thinking of Richard and Minna when (*Die Walküre*, Act II, Scene 2) Wotan behaves towards his lawfully wedded wife in exactly the same manner as an unfaithful and cowardly husband: he gives in when he should know better and show his character as a man. But later, when Brünnhilde is courageous and human and acts against his orders, he assumes the role of a vengeful Jehovah and debars his favourite daughter for ever from the community of the Gods.

At this point all grousing and all malicious fault-finding must come to a stop. It must be freely admitted that all preceding criticism is irrelevant. No listener with a modicum of human emotion will ever ponder about Wagner's inconsistencies and his dramatic cheating for one single moment. He will accept the lot because the emotional effect which this composer knows how to conjure up will silence all questions. It was for this reason that he always commanded the enthusiasm of his audience despite the music critics. What happens on stage has a logic of its own. It may be correct that in practical matters women are more clever than masculine warriors, but it is going a bit too far when, in the last scene of *Tristan*, the men are fighting to the bitter end for the gate of Kareol (with two major fatalities) whilst Brangäne, quite unconcernedly, jumps over the low wall to rush to the aid of her Mistress Isolde. We see this, but we take it in our stride. Such objections are in no way directed against the work as such, but only against the claim that it is the highest glory, the most holy, the irrevocably eternal dramatic art—directed against this phantasmagoria of the *Gesamtkunstwerk*. Whenever Wagner's effect is genuine and deeply sensed, it is an operatic effect and nothing else. If one accepts his work as that which it really is—as opera—then one also accepts all the melodramatic elements without contradiction and accepts all that one can find there: opera without equal. The dramatist and the musician worked hand in hand in an incomparable manner, and each gave to the other expressive possibilities such as never happened before. This positive achievement is the only true criterion for an evaluation of that Poet-Composer.

Many aspects in Wagner's works are dubious, and there are many contradictions: between what he strove for and what he has actually achieved, between the demands of his theories and the unwavering assurance of his artistic instinct. The pedantically conscientious dramatist loaded up his operatic cart with a ballast of theories, but in the event it became cruelly immaterial. Everything must be explained, must be motivated, and we are not spared one single detail of the possible pre-history. In that respect the *Ring* goes to the limit, which perhaps may be ascribed to its history (after all, the text was written in inverse order of concept), perhaps also to the fact that for performance purposes the four evenings were to be retained as independent entities. But it is a desperate business that in *Walküre* we have to sit through a complete recital of what has happened in *Rheingold*, and in *Siegfried* we have to listen to the whole lot again of what has happened in *Rheingold* and *Walküre*. In *Götterdämmerung*, to cap the matter, we have a recapitulation of everything that has happened in *Rheingold*, *Walküre* and *Siegfried*. All this would be tolerable if at least the music would remain at the same high level, but unfortunately this is not the case—in fact, it would be a major miracle if a composer had been able to chew the cud to such an extent and still remain inspired. Scenes such as the one between Wotan and Brünnhilde (*Walküre*, Act II) or the Wanderer-scene (*Siegfried*, Act I) are mere regurgitation of past history, devoid of invention, dessicated dialogues which are only sprinkled with *Leitmotive*. At moments such as these one realizes the wisdom of the *recitativo secco* in the old *opera seria*: it knew how to get rid of dialogue in the shortest possible space of time, and by its very negative musical content it gave spaciousness to the subsequent aria.

Such weaknesses are an integral part of the *Ring*, but there is a credit entry on the other side of the ledger which deserves honour and glory for its sheer monumentality. Anyone who could create this tetralogy was a giant, both in character and imperturbability of artistic vision. What is unique in this work is the curve of stylistic development which reflects a process of maturation encompassing twenty-five years, from its first conception in Dresden to its completion in Bayreuth. Probably this also accounts for the extraordinary stylistic differences of these four separate works which, basically, belong together. The beauty, the destiny in the maturing of this enormous conception is something which was not humanly "willed": it was something which developed unconsciously and which had the result that the progress from the forty-year-old to the sixty-year-old Wagner, from the primordial order of a world to its utter decline, went hand in hand with the progress from the primitive simplicity of *Rheingold* and its nature motives, from primary immediacy in which an untouched *Ur*-world seems to express itself, via the elementary and shattering storms of *Walküre* and the sun-lit heroic landscapes of *Siegfried*, to the immense peak of *Götterdämmerung*, jutting into the black menacing clouds, with its colossal, thematically basic motifs piled on top of each other as boulders into a unique finale, a towering monument. What happened to the musician, the actual centre of energy of his creativity, is that his artistic self-assurance had grown immeasurably in those two decades. This is reflected in the majesty of his *Götterdämmerung* style, in his polyphonic artistry, in the inexhaustible wealth of his harmonic and orchestral colourings. The many musical symbols, the *Leitmotive* which pervade this tetralogy—those of the Rhine Maidens, of the Gold, Valhalla, Wotan's Spear, Alberich's Curse and many others—are little more than a musical back-drop when they first appear in *Rheingold*, and in their highest, symphonic sense their thematic importance can as yet only be guessed at. It is only in *Götterdämmerung* that these motifs and their combinations develop into structures of incredibly impressive and expressive entities.

If *Götterdämmerung*, the most monumental work which Wagner ever created, is the external climax, then the emotional climax of the tetralogy is *Walküre*, the most humanly touching of the four dramas. The fate of Siegmund and Sieglinde, those two noble, passionate, unhappy persons whom Wotan has put into this world so senselessly and whom he then destroys equally senselessly, is unbelievably touching. And Wagner, who was the first to be affected and moved by their destiny, reached the height of one of his loftiest achievements with the music which he invented for them. It can be argued that the first act of *Walküre* is the most beautiful act of any opera of Wagner's creation. It is music of a tenderness, depth and an inner fire such as he himself never reached again. As has been mentioned, the tremendous development which leads from *Rheingold* to *Walküre* cannot be explained by a lapse of time, for the one was written immediately after the other. What does lie between them is an experience of fantasy, an experience of the dramatist, of which there is no comparable instance in the whole of Wagner's life. *Das Rheingold* is a fairy-tale: everything which happens in it is in the nature of a child's picture book, colourful and vivid, entertaining and eerie. In *Walküre* we are in a different realm, in the realm of genuine human tragedy. Siegmund and Sieglinde are simple human beings, created in order to live, but they are doomed by an inexorable fate, and their whole lives must fulfil themselves in the bliss of that one single night of spring which is the beginning of their ruin. The catastrophe at the end of Act II is preceded by a scene of overwhelming tragedy, when the Valkyrie appears to Siegmund to foretell his impending death—and when she, swayed by the irresistible

tempest of his emotions, throws caution to the winds and defies
Wotan's command. Seen side by side with this tragedy of living,
feeling humans, how sad a spectacle is Wotan with all his
power politics! Incidentally, once one accepts the absurdity of
all his actions, the drama itself has a classical impact and a
complete unity of line. And even more than that: it is a chain of
pictorial, exciting scenes which are beautifully moulded
dramatically as well as musically and are convincingly effective
as theatre—in other words: it is true opera.

This compliment—or this accusation, as Wagner would have
considered it—is the due of every one of his works, with one
exception: *Tristan und Isolde.* Here the artist has obeyed the
theoretician in the most logical manner. If one overlooks the
ineradicable melodramatic precepts, the dramatist has done
full justice in this work to the strictest demands of classical
drama. What the myth had to offer him was the fatal love
potion and the ministering Isolde who arrives too late to save
the life of the wounded Tristan. All the other ingredients were
Wagner's own. He cross-bred the pictorial motives of the legend
with Schopenhauer's philosophy (which occupied his thoughts
at the time) but in doing so he packed more abstract reflections
into the drama than the fairy-tale subject could absorb.
Inevitably this led to inflationary symptoms: in the first act it is
the never-ending narration in order to motivate the despair
which drives Isolde to the brink of the intended double suicide,
in the second the equally endless arguments to explain all that
is (and remains) absurd in Tristan's behaviour; and in the
third act it takes cruelly masochistic monologues on the part of
the mortally wounded Tristan, which finally lead to his death,
in order to illustrate the delay of Isolde's arrival in a dramatic
manner. (". . . that cannot be done so swiftly!") These may be
deficiencies, but they are also organic peculiarities of a work
which stands as it stands: a towering, unique achievement of
its kind. As Wagner himself suggested, it is possible to help
matters by discreet amputations in the first half of the great love
scene and in Act III, but this does not overcome the problems
of the whole work as such. Born out of a paroxysm of emotions
it can only live in a region of ecstasy which is not accessible to
someone with normal emotions unless on exceptional occasions.

Tristan and Isolde are standing on stilts, and their emotions are super-dimensional. By equating love and death, the tension is driven to extremes and as such pervades the whole. Even the off-stage sailor's song at the beginning of Act I sounds strangely unreal with its chromatic shifts; it is a characteristic detail from a different world of extravagant emotions, created out of sheer fantasy. Wagner saw this quite clearly when he wrote to Mathilde:

> I fear that the opera will be banned unless bad performances turn the whole into a parody: only mediocre performances can save me! Really good performances must drive people crazy—I cannot imagine it any other way.

Through *Lohengrin* the young Ludwig became addicted to Wagner, through *Tristan* a whole generation after him. Of all Wagner's fantastic attitudes, his Schopenhauer pose is the oddest. No other human being has ever been more fanatically driven by the urge of his will than he was, and now he goes and talks about overcoming the will by renunciation! But he believed, and he created. How deeply he had steeped himself in that fantastic passion can be gathered from the daily notes which he wrote in Venice for Mathilde: "Thus you dedicated yourself to death in order to give me life, and thus I received your life so that now I can leave this world with you, suffer with you, die with you!" As an artist he had a capability which transcends normal understanding to transmit the white heat of his fantasy straight into his work without any cooling off. It is difficult to judge *Tristan* as a work of art because, in actual fact, one can only love it or hate it, or at times both simultaneously. Cornelius was in what almost amounted to a state of panic, and he wrote to his fiancée:

> It is a great blow for Wagner that Ander in Vienna, who was diligently learning the part and probably almost knew it, had to die in mental derangement, and the actual performer [Schnorr] of typhus. Should one not accept this as a sign, as a warning that the bow which is to carry the arrow of enthusiasm into the hearts of the listeners has been drawn too

tautly? As a warning of this destructive art which ruthlessly and relentlessly churns up all fibres and nerves?

Anyone who is indifferent to *Tristan* lacks imagination. But what must be considered as the criterion of an evaluation is the tremendous fact that Wagner has created a style of unique individuality, and that he has unlocked the door to melodic and harmonic secrets which no one before him had even guessed at.

Even if one does not allow oneself to become completely submerged in this work, there will nevertheless remain two episodes in the overall impression which are unparalleled in dramatic music as far as the shattering intensity of the experience is concerned. Both belong to the mortally wounded Tristan— how Wagner must have identified himself with Tristan's suffering! Racked by fever, he listens to the mournful tune of the shepherd which then is taken over by the orchestra and spun out, and his entire life, as in a dream, passes before his eyes against this background, based on the *cantus firmus* of this piercing, tormenting, this unspeakably terrifying melody. Difficult to say whether this is still music, this expression of a sick soul clothed in musical garb. The other episode comes later, when he regains consciousness and has a fevered vision of the ship on which Isolde is approaching. The way in which the four horns at this point paraphrase a lyrical passage from the love duet of Act II, from an expression of calm tenderness to the most exuberant rapture, how against this music Tristan's singing becomes ever more intense until it culminates in the ecstatic shout "Isolde, how fair art thou!", and how finally, when the emotional temperature reaches boiling point, the shepherd spots Isolde's ship and his joyous tune rings out—this is beautiful music, but it is impossible to do justice to the effect of this scene from a purely musical point of view. Here it is truly the drama, the unity of the visual and the musical expression together with our deeply involved feelings, which communicates an artistic experience of such intensity.

Little purpose would be served in analysing the means by which the magician Wagner obtained such effects. Musicians who are interested in the matter will have to search the secrets of the subsidiary dominants, through which all the semitone intervals of the chromatic scale are brought into a diatonic and tonal connection. But so much nonsense has been written about Wagnerian harmony, especially as regards *Tristan*, that perhaps it is not superfluous to point out that, although Wagner explored the most subtle potentials of tonality and forced them into his service, he never left the gravitational field of the tonic key by as much as a hair's breadth. We even find something in Wagner which applies to all of Mozart's operas as well as to Weber's *Freischütz*, *Euryanthe* and *Oberon*: that an entire opera has its individual tonic key which encompasses the whole work from beginning to end and creates a clearly audible unification. This is the case in *Lohengrin* (A major), in *Die Meistersinger* (C major) and in *Parsifal* (A flat major). Although apparently it is not evident to everyone, Wagner himself answered the question of tonality quite unambiguously by composing a concert ending for the *Tristan* Prelude which ends in A major, the categorical consequence of a tonality which has A as its basis—even though, by the fact that the harmonic progressions always come close to this centre of gravity without ever reaching it, this tonality, this tonic A, becomes the symbol of an eternal, unfulfilled yearning. It is utter rubbish to take *Tristan*, the most comprehensive consequence of tonal style, as the basis of an argument to prove the necessity of a development towards atonality. Wagner made his arduous way with an infallible sense of direction, and one cannot hold him responsible for the fact that others following him were partially blind and lost the track. His music is strongly inspired and determined by drama, but exigencies of expression or tone-poem tendencies never impinged on his sense for the integrity of musical interrelations. There is not one note in a Wagner score which is not unequivocally determined by the musical context. It is true that he stirred up the biggest confusion in the whole of musical history (here he is guilty as a theorist, innocent as a musician), that he unbalanced a whole generation of composers, and that many of those that came after him succumbed to the temptation of living harmonically beyond their means. Of course since then the disaster has gone further, and long ago we have arrived at a revolt of a great majority, the unmusical of all nations, against music itself. What has changed course by 180 degrees, however, is public opinion. At the time of *Tristan* the Hanslicks were grousing, while the public in their thousands followed Wagner like another Pied Piper of Hamelin. Today it is the other way round: the public stays at home when it comes to the latest thing produced on tape and leaves the enthusing to the critics, who have learnt from Hanslick's example that one cannot be too cautious. There is only one thing which they overlook: that even caution needs some controlling intelligence.

It is proof of Wagner's thoroughly healthy nature that out of the ecstasy and the chromatic twilight of *Tristan* he could escape into the brightest down-to-earth world in which he ever set foot. This demanded time and a considerable change in his external circumstances. Wagner, so dominated by the force of his own will, really had to bestir himself, had to come to grips with the world, had to gain new experiences, and the Paris *Tannhäuser* fiasco as well as the restlessness and upheavals that preceded and followed that period saw to all that. In the *Tannhäuser* Bacchanale which he wrote in Paris one can notice that he still had the *Tristan* bug in his blood. It obviously needed a stronger and more decisive impulse to revitalize his creative forces and to direct them into channels which his instinct would tell him were the right ones. And so, almost by accident, he found, at the back of his consciousness, the *Meistersinger* subject for which he had made sketches in Dresden sixteen years earlier.

Die Meistersinger did not turn into the light comic opera which Wagner at the time had promised his publishers, just as *Tristan* could never become, as once intended, an Italian opera to suit the taste of Rio de Janeiro. Wagner's utterance has its specific breadth and weightiness; the gift of writing in a lighter vein was denied him. When, at the age of eighty, his great counterpart Verdi gave the world his *Falstaff*, he also had undergone that miraculous mutation by which an artist who has devoted his life to the tragic muse arrives at a new outlook on life in comedy. Falstaff's greatest charm is his ability to take everything easily in his stride, and the text of his final fugue *Tutto nel mondo è burla* is a philosophy, a *Weltanschauung* in itself. But *Die Meistersinger* was composed a quarter of a century earlier. Wagner still had to bear the undiminished burden which, whether one liked it or not, was part and parcel of the world of romantic emotions and its fancy dress, and it was a *sine qua non* of the romantic to take himself and those emotions seriously. The first bars of the *Meistersinger* Prelude with their weighty pompousness leave no room for doubt that what follows will be a glorious event, with nothing comic about it. *Die Meistersinger* is far too serious and too pointedly ideological to be a comedy; it is a dramatic plea *pro domo*, satire and self-glorification rolled into one, a unique fusion of proclamation, drama and opera.

There can be no doubt, this is a real opera. The theorist on questions of music drama must have had to close both eyes very firmly. In its whole lay-out, and despite all disavowal, this work with its broadly conceived musical episodes, with its spotlights on the protagonists and its large-scale finales follows the indestructible ideals of that form of opera which the wisdom of generations had brought into being. Here the immediate musical possibilities of the subject, from which the Minstrels' Contest on the Wartburg had profited so little, reaped the richest of harvests, with Walter's Prize Song as the most beautiful blossom of Wagnerian lyricism. And—surprise, surprise!—the opera composer even succeeded in extracting a small ballet scene out of the stern and severe dramatist, the Dance of the Apprentices, that charming and delightful introduction to the scene on the *Festwiese*. Of the deeply-rooted habits of the music-dramatist *Die Meistersinger* has inherited nothing but the immense breadth of representation without which Wagner simply could not express himself; but actually there are only three episodes in the whole work in which the dampening effect of lengthy prosaic dialogue has made life difficult for the opera composer. In the first instance it is the assembly of the Masters in Act I which has already been mentioned, then Hans Sachs' long and involved theoretical explanation of poetic art which he gives to Walter in his cobbler's workshop, and finally the completely unnecessary precision with which he tells the assembled crowd of the *Festwiese* what is about to come: we have all known it for a long time, and presumably so has the assembled citizenry of

Nürnberg. But this is far less ballast than we normally encounter in Wagner and, disregarding those three scenes, there is hardly one tedious length in *Meistersinger*: it is a triumph of the richest, never-ending spring of invention.

While he was working on the composition, music must have surged forth out of every one of Wagner's pores. Perhaps it all resulted from a cause of which he himself was unaware: the sheer joy of being free from that shrouded world of mythology with its sombre draperies (preferably of satin and brocade), its gods and heroes, giants and dwarfs, its love potions and magic helmets; free, just for once, to deal with real beings, real feelings, real facts, with human beings with whom one can laugh or weep, whom one can love or hate. And how well those human beings have fared in the process! Eva is Wagner's most natural and poetic female character, Walter Stolzing his only hero who combines romantic extravaganza with some *Gemütlichkeit* and even a spark of humour, and Hans Sachs with his wealth of humanity, his indestructible natural common sense, is one of the immortal characters of the stage of all times.

Die Meistersinger drew much profit from a shift of the centre of gravity which occurred in the period between the original sketch and the final composition. At the time of the first draft, when Wagner was thirty, he identified himself with Walter Stolzing, that artist of innate genius, who opposed the ridiculous conventions of the Masters with the full consciousness of his superiority and the conviction of what he considered his due. By the time he returned to this draft, at the age of fifty, he was a master himself before the whole world. Now it was Hans Sachs with whom he identified, and he poured into this character all the wealth, all the nobility which his imagination could conceive. This dual personal relationship has the result that the two chief protagonists who continuously face each other, Walter and Sachs, are of life-like vitality, and it gives the whole opera a heart-warming reality such as can hardly ever be found elsewhere in Wagner. His self-glorification, too, is such a natural expression of an extremely egocentric personality that no trace of vanity makes itself felt—and this egocentric nature of his obviously did not allow him to notice how much he had sinned against this ideal of his—Sachs—when he took Cosima. Hans Sachs was in a similar position, but with noble resignation, after earnest heart-searchings, he renounced Eva. . . .

Apart from the main protagonists the subsidiary characters are also drawn with an unsurpassable love of detail. If one compares kind Papa Pogner with his predecessor Daland of *Der fliegende Holländer*—for in operatic convention they represent the same type of role—one recognizes immediately how much progress the dramatist had made since those early days. In the same way the "second pair of lovers" of conventional opera, David and Magdalene, are anything but mere pattern: they are individuals, bubbling over with vitality. It is only when one compares the character types of *Die Meistersinger* with those of the *Ring* that the enormous contrast becomes obvious. Earlier it has been pointed out that the intriguers and antagonists of the *Ring* suffer from what might be called a constitutional poverty of musical invention, and the same applies to *Lohengrin*, *Tristan*, *Parsifal*. In *Meistersinger* no single figure on stage suffers from this sort of anaemia, and even Kothner, that sober head of the guild, gets his shimmer of musical glory when he reads out the tabulature. As to Beckmesser, the "Marker": this incarnation of non-art and non-feeling is an original and a personality. Nothing is cheaper than parody, and this character could so easily have turned into nothing but farce—but Wagner wisely restricted the parodistic elements in Beckmesser to discreet innuendoes. His serenade is a masterpiece: despite and, at the same time, because of its parodistic details it is a magnificent melodic invention, blessed with a rhythmic charm of its own, out of which could later grow the whole wonderful structure of the Finale of Act II. Exasperated to the utmost by Sachs' drastic "marking" with the hammer on his last, Beckmesser finally staggers breathlessly through his last verse—then David goes for him because, with the undimmed eyesight of a young lad, he has recognized that, though dressed up as Eva, it was Magdalene sitting by the window, and of course he assumes that the serenade was meant for her. This starts a glorious general fight, and in the end nobody really knows any longer who is hitting whom, or why. The *Prügelmotiv* (the "Brawl Motif") which is struck up by the orchestra develops into a fugue, to which Beckmesser's serenade melody contributes the counter-subject. This tune, rising by thirds, drives the music upwards and upwards until it reaches its climax (and that is the whole purpose of the procedure) on F sharp, the one and only note on the night-watchman's horn which had been heard once before in the preceding scene. The note of that horn is a signal for general panic, and the crowd scatters in a twinkling in all directions. At the same time this note gives rise to a most beautiful melody to which earlier Walter and Eva had listened under the linden tree, a melody which breathes all the poetic magic of a midsummer night. Then the night-watchman makes his entry. Drowsy with sleep he sings his song and is convinced that all the rumpus which he heard from afar was nothing but a dream. The orchestra picks up the midsummer-night melody; it is interrupted by reminiscences of the *Prügelmotiv* and interspersed by fragments of Beckmesser's serenade until the curtain falls—the most wonderful ending to an act which opera has ever known:

Brahms respected Wagner, but he always remained a cool and critical judge of his famous contemporary. As a charming and spontaneous sign of his acknowledgment he involuntarily quoted this ending in one of his late piano pieces (Op. 119, no. 2) and it is interesting to note that here, as in many similar cases, the identity of tonality points clearly to a subconscious memory. (See page 189.)

But there is another *nota bene* which cannot be avoided: the

joyousness of this finale is impaired by the fact that in the *Prügel*-scene the vocal parts sound terrible. To an expert a single glance at the vocal score makes the reason obvious:

Despite the very lively tempo, Wagner articulated and phrased the vocal lines as though he were dealing with instruments. His intuitive feel for orchestral sonority was infallible, and it is strange how much he lacked in this respect when it came to the vocal forces. In the case of a dramatic solo voice he was exceedingly sensitive to expressive declamation, but in ensembles he always succumbed to the temptation of demanding things of the human voice for which it simply is not made. There are chorus masters who will proudly declare that their choir can sing the *Prügel*-scene correctly without accompaniment. In the rehearsal room, perhaps! But never on stage, where the end result is never more than chaotic shouting. At best this shouting is in time, but it is never particularly pretty to listen to. Some may say that, when everybody is hitting everybody else anyway, this does not matter very much—but it is questionable whether the resultant general bellowing is worth the infinite and meticulous labour which went into it at rehearsals.

Fortunately Wagner can write differently too, and in his *Meistersinger* he has given proof of it. Of the many misguided dicta of his theory perhaps the most astounding is his preparedness to forgo one of the most beautiful possibilities of operatic style, the vocal ensemble. In the *Ring* as in *Tristan* he had adhered to a principle with only negligible exceptions, the principle which Hanslick has described as a "vocal game of follow-my-leader". In *Meistersinger* he threw his theory overboard. He did not go so far as to allow scenes such as that between Eva and Walter, or between Sachs and Eva, to degenerate into a duet; but when he is urged by the warmth of his feelings, when Walter's new-born Master Song is to be baptized, he brings together the five participants of this scene in a quintet which spreads a radiance of glory over the whole work: it is the emotional climax as opposed to the external climax on the *Festwiese*. At times one may lose patience with Wagner when he gets too long-winded. But when the action comes to a deeply-moving event and emotion to a concentrated utterance, then the music is crystallized and becomes unique, incomparable. In the *Meistersinger*-Quintet the composer draws the operatic conclusion from an operatic situation, and it even happens to him that he makes use of a form which since Rossini had become a staple part of every Italian opera and which was the simplest manner of shaping an operatic ensemble. In actual fact this form is Rossini's own creation, the consequence of a style in which melody is the be-all and end-all. These ensembles begin in the manner of an aria, with a broad melody sung by the leading voice; one by one the other voices come in in the course of a slightly contrasting middle section which, with increasing expressiveness, leads to the recapitulation of the original melody which now, supported by the whole ensemble, works up to a climax. It is difficult to imagine a more primitive form-principle, but it is irresistibly effective with beautiful voices and a beautiful melody, the essence of everything which Italian opera has to offer. In the *Meistersinger*-Quintet Wagner unashamedly puts this form to use, which shows his lack of prejudice when it comes to the crunch—but also that, when it comes to inventing a melody, he is everybody's match, provided he is involved heart and soul.

When he was in his fifties, at the time of *Meistersinger*, he felt himself at the peak of his creative powers. At sixty he completed the *Ring*, "the colossal work" as he himself described it. He then had the conviction that his vitality was inexhaustible and felt himself as one of the Chosen. At that time he wrote to Pusinelli:

> As to my health, it would appear—particularly to the specialists—that I am an example of a special type of human species, destined to long life and labours. . . . I need much time, for everything I write down is in the superlative.

And to his publishers Schott:

> I am confident that fate has sturdy health and great age with a youthful spirit in store for me, so that just for once someone may accomplish and experience something for which normally in Germany one needs two life-spans.

Without his last fantastic adventure, Bayreuth, which wore him out, this prediction could possibly have come true. A glance at the *Parsifal* score discloses what had happened to him during those years: that score is an autumnal landscape with dead leaves, hoar-frost on the ground, with hardly a trace of sunshine. This music has something venerable in its touching genuineness, in the uncompromising severity of its style and in its incomparably wise disposition of colours. But it is the music of a tired and exhausted man which lacks the very factor which had always been at the root of Wagner's magic: the eruptive inspiration. This Holy Grail is a shapeless, nebulous something compared with that other Grail which, thirty years earlier and "in distant lands, to mortal feet forbidden", had been Lohengrin's symbol of salvation. It may have been an instinctive feeling of this nature which caused the young Ludwig (cf. p. 102) to request a performance of the *Lohengrin* Prelude as a comparison. Wagner must have felt somehow offended, and this could explain the irritation with which he reacted to the whim of his King. In *Parsifal* everything seems to be a little bit second-hand, even though this "second hand" is still the hand of a master. In the Prelude the motif of the Last Supper first appears in unison and then in full orchestral array: the harmonies are not of this earth, the sound as a whole is celestial— yet the vital sap, the blessing of inspiration, is missing. Apart from a few lively bars when Parsifal makes his first appearance and which remain his *Leitmotiv*, this blessing of inspiration is absent right up to the finale of an interminably long first act, two-thirds of which, in any case, are taken up by the immoderately garrulous Gurnemanz, the ever-annotating factotum of the work. Then comes the finale which has the nobility of a great cathedral, even though here again the main effectiveness rests on the vast calm of the structural planes.

By comparison with the static first act, which is almost entirely dedicated to exposition, Act II is again true opera with Wagner's unerring sense of dramatic tension and climax. Unfortunately even here the most decisive scene, Kundry's seductive blandishments, suffers a setback because it is overladen with explanatory text—once again the dramatist has broken the flow of the opera composer. As up to that point we have not yet heard anything of Parsifal's personal background, it is now up to Kundry to inform us about his past history, and like an elderly aunt she tells him all about his ancestry and childhood. The stream of the music gets lost in a bog of tediousness, and Parsifal remains unseduced. The musical highlight of this act is the scene of the Flower Maidens, music of sparkling freshness, the material of which may well belong to an earlier period. This also applies to the solemn Good Friday scene in the third act. It is the beginning of the most momentous section of the entire work, the great final apotheosis in which particularly the strong contrast with the scene in the Temple of the Grail at the end of Act I is an imposing achievement. What makes it so difficult to accept *Parsifal* with complete and sympathetic conviction is the slow pulse of this music, which is a farewell, an ending, a monument of unshakeable artistic integrity. The *Gesamtkunstwerk* has turned into the *Weihefestspiel*, the "Solemn Festival Drama", and Wagner well knew why he wanted performances restricted to Bayreuth.

When in 1913 *Parsifal* came out of copyright there was no way of preventing opera houses all over the world from taking possession of it, but it never became a repertoire work: performances are still restricted to rare occasions, and *Parsifal* is and remains an object of respectful veneration, but hardly of love.

G

5

ETERNAL OPERA

HISTORY HAS PRONOUNCED its verdict on Wagner as a reformer. He succeeded in establishing himself as Pope, but he did not found a new church, and his great theoretical edifice which was no less radical than Luther's Ninety-five Theses is now nothing but an historical curiosity. What is such a paradox is that Wagner, who set out to destroy opera, is precisely the man who, for decades to come, gave opera its best repertoire pieces and thereby did more for its continued existence than anyone else. It has been mentioned in passing that this circumstance—which already had become noticeable during his lifetime—aroused conflicting emotions in him. Whenever he "surrendered" (as he called it) a work to the theatres he felt humiliated, and the money which he got for it he threw out of the window as quickly as he possibly could. Then, when his work was successful in that profane world, he was happy almost against his own will. He was certainly justified in accusing the average operatic institution of a humdrum, routine insufficiency as regards both the stage and the orchestra pit, and against this he battled heroically in Dresden. It was difficult for any theatre to satisfy him when it came to his own works, and after a *Lohengrin* performance under von Bülow he commented:

> Only once did I have the opportunity in Munich to rehearse my work according to my intentions, at least as concerns its rhythmic and architectural structure. Anyone who witnessed the performances which here resulted from true feeling and understanding can now only be amazed at one thing: that it was a matter of utter indifference to the audience whether they saw *Lohengrin* in this way or another. When later the opera was given again in the old routine, the impression it made still remained the same.

And he concludes in despair:

> All your conductors from A to Z cannot conduct my operas,
> because at best they are only routine musicians who know
> and understand nothing—but nothing!—of the theatre apart
> from the bad habits of all this opera singing. No, a different
> man is now needed! In any case, I am by now fed up in every
> respect and am firmly resolved never again to lend a helping
> hand to any theatre. The way in which everything is run is
> so fatuous, and a man like myself simply cannot have
> anything to do with it.

But then, despite himself, he is greatly impressed when he
hears such a routine performance and realizes how, in spite of
everything, the essence of the work still comes across, simply
because it is strong enough to make its impact felt under all
circumstances:

> Just a few words to let you know that yesterday I had the
> good fortune to hear my *Lohengrin* for the first time, and not only
> that, but also in a performance which has moved and pleased
> me equally. At the same time the Vienna public gave me an
> ovation such as, so they say, no composer has ever received
> here: I was shattered that such enthusiasm should be possible.
> Everything, the greatest riches with which atonement can
> be made to an artist for every privation he has undergone, all
> the ill-treatment he has suffered, were lavished upon me, so
> that my heart is consoled to its very depth.

Or, after *Tristan* in Munich:

> It was the German public which always supported me against
> the most peculiar hostilities of factions, and I may also
> confidently put my trust in the Munich audiences.

Not without some amusement he reports about a performance
of *Rheingold* which, at the order of the King, had taken place in
Munich against his will and during his absence:

I had to suffer great annoyance over this affair in Munich, but strangely it could not efface the impression which ultimately it had on me. It made me realize that this most difficult part of the cycle, namely *Das Rheingold*, cannot be murdered even in a basically nonsensical and certainly dull and uninspired performance. On the contrary, it has proved its effectiveness with the audience, so that several theatres are now considering including it in their repertoire.

One single circumstance can explain all the contradictions, all the ambiguities of impressions, emotions, comments: the magic of the theatre. This magic has made possible that most erratic of all art forms—opera, has preserved it through the course of centuries and has given it a life force which could withstand even Wagner's most embittered attacks. Opera is a freak, being the result of seemingly irreconcilable presuppositions, but the freak lives. There can hardly be any doubt that Wagner's works have survived, not because they are "music dramas", but because they are operas. He began his career as an opera composer, and as an opera *Kapellmeister* he gathered his first practical experience. The flair for operatic effects was ineradicably in his blood. When he started on his aesthetic and philosophical artistic speculations, and the idea of the *Gesamtkunstwerk* began to mature, he found himself caught for ever after in a cleft stick between his radical theories and the inexterminable instinct of a full-blooded musician. The opera composer in him fought a defensive action against music drama, and one is tempted to say that it was a battle of the artist against the pedant.

It was a tremendous advantage for Wagner to be his own librettist, and a librettist of exceptional talent at that, but it certainly also led to his over-estimation of the dramatist *en face* the composer—and from there onwards to the peremptory tenet that he himself was the Chosen One to solve this problem. Had it not been so, he could not have failed to see that the ideal musico-dramatic effect had been attained long ago, even if only in exceptional cases of blessed inspiration. Only a megalomaniac could all but ignore Mozart's great operas, Beethoven's *Fidelio*, Gluck's *Orfeo*, Weber's *Freischütz*, Rossini's *Barbiere*, and granting them nothing except some good points (and that condescendingly!), stress the basic ailment with which the whole species was irrevocably tainted.

The whole history of opera, its eternal oscillation between the dramatic and the musical idea, teaches us that these problems cannot be solved by any theory, and it is precisely Wagner, the indomitable theorist, who has given us a valuable contribution towards understanding this. In order to survive, an opera must come into being through the happy meeting of a passable libretto, inspired music and a relationship between these two components resulting in a perfect equilibrium of stage effect and musical effect. But this equilibrium is dependent, first and foremost, on the vocal impression. In spoken drama it is the living, loving, suffering, laughing, weeping, moving human being and his destiny who is decisive for our sympathy or otherwise. In opera it is the *singing* person: the more perfect the transmutation of a character into a voice, and the more beautiful the voice, the more immediate the effect. From the very beginnings of opera the charm of beautiful voices has been its main attraction, and parallel with its development the Italian art of singing has grown and become what it has been since the end of the seventeenth century and has remained to this day. Opera and *bel canto* are one and the same, the most beautiful afterglow of the Renaissance. French opera, much though it later developed in its own peculiar manner, was directly inspired by Italian models. German opera, like all German cultural life, was long held back by the aftermath of the Thirty Years' War and so was the last to arrive on the scene, and really it was only with Mozart's *Zauberflöte* that it truly came into its own as a fully-fledged art-form. But like the Renaissance, opera drew its greatest strength from international cross-currents. An Italian, Lully, was the founder of French opera; a German, Händel, was the greatest master of Italian baroque opera; as an opera composer Mozart was at least half an Italian; and Beethoven's *Fidelio*, written to a text which was originally French, is both technically and stylistically indebted to the French operas of Cherubini, an Italian. A fanatical nationalism such as Wagner's simply ignores the very basic facts of operatic history. Anyone who condemns opera for being "un-German" may just as well condemn Bach's polyphony because it is of Netherlandish origin, or the dance forms of his Suites because he borrowed them from France, or Beethoven's symphonies because their ancestors were Italians.

Wagner was by no means the originator of the aggressive inferiority complex of the German opera composer. Weber himself was not free of it with his passionate counter-attacks on Rossini who was so victorious on all German stages. What German opera lacked so desperately after Weber's premature death in 1826 was the guiding spirit of genius. Spohr and Marschner, the acknowledged masters of the 1830s, have long since vanished from our stages, apart from rare attempts at revival. On the other hand their far more unassuming con- temporary Lortzing has successfully held his own in Germany, thanks to his blessed humour and his natural simplicity, but perhaps above all to his infallible sense of the theatre, which he —in his modest way also a poet-composer—shared with Wagner. It is significant that in his analysis of opera Wagner never so much as mentions Lortzing's name, althought he must have known his works (Lortzing lived in Leipzig during the days of Wagner's youth) and without any doubt he was inspired in his subject matter by one Lortzing opera: it is called *Hans Sachs*. Lortzing had no literary ambition—metaphorically speaking he wrote his texts with his coat off, in shirt-sleeves—and this probably made it impossible for Wagner even to take notice of him. Now it certainly is an advantage if, apart from its other qualities, an opera text also conforms to certain literary standards, and it is one of Wagner's great merits that in this respect he has made the librettist's conscience more sensitive. Nevertheless the fact that, despite Wagner's life-long efforts, so many operas which in terms of literary merit are not worthy of consideration can still maintain their place in the repertoire, speaks against the assumption that a decisive importance must be ascribed to this. Meyerbeer, it is true, has vanished from the stage, but to that end he hardly needed the push which Wagner gave him.

Meyerbeer craved for effects, but this was the least of his vices, for it is an old portion of opera. In its beginnings, as the costly entertainment of princely patrons, *décor*, machinery and precious costumes formed part of its indispensable requisites, and this tendency was preserved in Paris where opera stood under the immediate patronage of the king; hence Spontini's and Meyerbeer's predilection for scenic pomp was in absolute accordance with tradition. Nor did Wagner disdain the use of such operatic means of effectiveness. This not only applies to *Rienzi* which, in any case, is based on the French pattern throughout, but to just about all his other works with the sole exception of *Tristan* which became a true "drama of the soul" as Wagner called it. The arrival of the Dutchman's ship in the *Holländer*, the *Venusberg* and the hunt (complete with baying of hounds and twelve blaring horns) in *Tannhäuser*, the arrival of Lohengrin with his swan, the duel and the procession to the Minster in *Lohengrin*—all these are scenic moments of effectiveness borrowed from *grand opéra*. It is the same thing with the whole of the *Ring*, from the capricious unreality of the Rhine Maidens, the fairy-tale world of Nibelheim, Donners' thunder magic and the rainbow bridge in *Rheingold* right up to the destruction of the Hall of the Gibichungs and the burning of Valhalla in the final scene of *Götterdämmerung*. When it comes to that, Meyerbeer did nothing more contemptible with the jaws of hell in *Robert le Diable*, the sunrise in *Le Prophète* or the shipwreck in *L'Africaine* than Wagner did all his life in order to build up the action of the opera towards climactic moments of scenic impressiveness. It is one of the many problems of opera that so often the visual effect has to step in and supply what the word lacks in clarity: we have to see in order to understand. In any concept of opera it is of great importance that it works towards an impressive visual effect, and Wagner always acted in accordance with this precept, even though he says little about it in his theoretical writings. When he prepared the *Ring* for its first Bayreuth performance, the engineer working the stage machinery was just as important to him as the conductor, and he spared no trouble and no expense to get the best to be had for his stage *décor*, even if he was not always successful. By mistake part of the dragon for *Siegfried* which had been ordered in London and which had to be transported in sections ended up in Beirut instead of Bayreuth, where it only arrived months too late. From earliest days onwards Wagner took all matters concerned with *décor* very seriously, and for the *Tannhäuser* performance in Dresden, just to give an example, he insisted on a very expensive set for the Minstrels' Hall which had to be got from Paris. He knew only too well how much the success of a performance depended on such external super-ficialities. But these apparent superficialities were also part of his very individually disposed imagination, in visual as in musical respects. His own stage directions, terse, wisely directed to the essentials, can well demand to be observed as meticulously by the producer as the notes and dynamic markings by the conductor.

It is obvious that the singer should also observe both, but strangely it is precisely the Wagner tradition, the "Bayreuth Style", which has fostered mannerisms of singing which in no way correspond to what the Master must have intended when he wrote his scores. Anyone who looks through a Wagner vocal score will find that everywhere in the vocal parts there are certain *legato* ties which join broad singing phrases and are in cross contradiction to what many Wagner interpreters custom-arily do. Clearly and without ambiguity the composer indicated the difference between dramatic declamation and lyrical *legato* singing, in *Tristan* as in the *Ring* and in *Meister-singer*—even in *Lohengrin* where, apparently, he first realized the necessity of making this distinction. Of course we do not know how he himself handled these matters. Considering how obsessed he was with clarity of articulation he himself may partially be to blame for those usages which have compromised the Wagner style to a certain extent. What Camille Saint-Saëns, a faithful Wagner adherent from the time of the *Tannhäuser* days in Paris, has to say about the first Bayreuth Festival of 1876 allows the conclusion that beauty of singing was the last quality to arouse admiration, for he adds: "Singers who deserve that name are rare in Germany; most of those who participated in the *Ring* screamed rather than sang." Vocal training may have much improved since that time, but a Wagnerian singer with a real *legato* is still a rare bird, for that demands true singing culture, faultless breath control, and an iron determination not to allow oneself to be driven to exag-geration, not even by the most voluptuous orchestral sound.

From many of his comments we know that a beautifully sounding voice was an aim for which Wagner always longed, but it is equally well known that often he had to make do with what he considered the lesser evil: clarity of diction at the expense of vocal beauty.

He himself, of course, would never have admitted that it was he who was at the root of that evil. Throughout all his writings he stresses—it is almost like a *Leitmotiv*!—his demands for an expressive, correctly accentuated declamation. It is this which he misses in Mozart, in Beethoven, in Weber, and he ascribes it to the circumstance that to date a fundamentally German style of singing just has not yet been found. As in many of his other presuppositions he was wrong here as well. Quite apart from the fact that since the seventeenth century there had always been a true German style of singing, there was also at least one amongst those closer to him in time, a child of his century, who had preceded him: Franz Schubert. Naturally, the aims of Wagner's vocal style were completely different. He demanded a dramatic pathos which was worlds removed from Schubert just as, on the other hand, he had only a very limited talent for that relaxed lyrical vocal phrase in which Schubert was so inexhaustible. Whenever, for reasons of dramatic style, he had to fall back on the traditional lyrical *cantabile* as in *Rienzi* and still in certain sections of *Der fliegende Holländer*—Daland, Erik—his inspiration was second-hand, whereas the impetuous declamation of the Dutchman and Senta's passionate ecstasy were forms of expression which came much more naturally to him. But, generally speaking, Wagner's orchestral invention is more original and more individual than his vocal melodies, and the entire development of his style must have been influenced by this. Wagner always delighted in presenting his works to his friends, with Liszt, Bülow, Tausig at the piano and himself as the singer, and those who were witnesses on such occasions have high praise for the vivacity and intensity of his performances. He therefore must certainly have had a high measure of sensibility for vocal articulation, but apparently his urge for expressiveness was above all directed towards a meaningful declamation.

This predominantly declamatory style of singing is the

"point of no return" between opera and music drama. In opera it was restricted to the recitative, a *parlando* accompanied by the orchestra only for punctuation which had the purpose of giving information and which could only in certain more excited moments move from an objective to a dramatically accentuated note. By the principle of leaving the musical reins to the orchestra for long stretches, Wagner enlarged the effective range of the declamatory style immensely without, despite all his efforts, having rendered any conspicuous service to the comprehensibility of the words: that, no matter what one does, remains a pious hope. Nothing is clearer than that a musician, for as long as he adheres strictly to this declamatory style, binds himself hand and foot as far as his freedom of invention is concerned, for as the ultimate result he finds that he is scanning instead of singing. But even here there are differences: Erda's chant in *Rheingold*, Siegmund's *Ein Schwert verhiess mir der Vater* ("A sword once promised my father"), Brünnhilde's *War es so schmählich* ("Was it so shameful") are true flashes of characteristic inventions within this style, but elsewhere (and only too often!) music has to sacrifice itself for the dramatic effect and do penance. We are lucky that Wagner's urge for dramatic effect is countered by his healthy sense of opera, his delicate instinct for the moment where the course of the dramatic action is in need of a lyrical oasis. This instinct leads him, even within the dramatic situation itself, to find the right moment for such insertions— Siegfried's forging songs, Stolzing's *Am stillen Herd* ("By silent hearth"), the cobbler's song of Hans Sachs—nor does he shun such pure lyricism as Siegmund's "Winter storms", the lilac monologue of Sachs or the quintet in the third act of *Meistersinger* which has already been discussed. Even the immensely broad development of the love dialogue between Tristan and Isolde in the end cannot help blossoming forth as a duet.

Apart from its purely lyrical opening (*O sink hernieder, Nacht der Liebe*) it is difficult to be really at ease when listening to this great duet. The reason is that, as has been mentioned earlier, Wagner's feeling for vocal sound does not come up to his infallible sense of orchestral sonorities, and in this respect curious things can happen to him. The white heat which this duet reaches leads to a tension of intervals which are of absurd ugliness. A vocal composer knows that the intervals of vocal parts will never fuse into one chord with their instrumental accompaniment, but will stand out exposed and naked. If, as is the case in the following phrase, the two voices keep meeting on the interval of a seventh, no harmonic padding of the orchestra can make any difference—the singers will lose their assurance and the seventh will become turgid to the point of harmonic incomprehensibility.

Actually Wagner's tendency to whip his singers into paroxysms of passion is a danger in itself, because there is a sort of acoustic saturation point beyond which singing ceases to be singing. This applies not only to Tristan and Isolde, but also to Siegfried and Brünnhilde in the last act of *Siegfried* when the hero and the demi-goddess (another one of those pairs of super-dimensional lovers) are egging each other on in their vocal excesses which in the end result in the grotesque instead of the sublime. Is it really necessary? Perhaps not. But there is a penalty for shifting the centre of gravity into the orchestra, and for a singer the need to prove his mettle against such a welter of sound bursting forth from the pit gives rise to an almost irresistible urge for the most desperate of counter-measures. No-one understood this better than that great and practical man of opera, Richard Wagner. When, in the spring of 1881, Angelo Neumann gave the first Berlin performance of the *Ring*

with his ensemble, he quoted the following words from an
address which Wagner himself gave to the orchestra:

> Gentlemen, please, don't take the *fortissimo* too seriously, and
> where I have written it, turn it into a *forte-piano*, and a *piano*
> into a *pianissimo*. Please remember that there are so many of
> you down here, and up there only one solitary human throat.

These are words which every Wagner conductor should bear in
mind.

The greatest evil of orchestral opera is that, in a manner of
speaking, it distorts the perspective. In the theatre our attention is riveted to the stage, and the character on stage will only
become a living reality if we can accept him or her as the
focal point of the music. Wagner was too much of an opera
composer to break this law continually, and even when he shifts
this focal point into the orchestra he knows how to preserve the
necessary flowing continuity of the declamation in the vocal line.
A classic example is Isolde, dying: she stands in contrast to the
symphonically self-contained orchestral sound as a soul already
transcended into higher spheres. Technically speaking she is a
mere contrapuntal, subsidiary line. It is most awkward to have to
admit that the *Liebestod* can also be performed as a concert item
without the vocal part, which thereby is proved to be a super-
numerary.

One must go back to the classics of opera to track down the
truth. When we think of a Mozart opera it is living personalities
of character who come to mind immediately: Figaro and
Susanna, Don Giovanni and Leporello, Tamino, Sarastro,
Papageno—right down to the little Barbarina in *Figaro* who,
even she, is already a fully fashioned, unmistakeable personality.
If one reads the libretto they are all meagre *dramatis personae*,
character sketches, stereotypes, but the music has breathed the
breath of life into them. Every true opera composer must also
be a poet. He creates a masterpiece to a text, the main function
of which is to incite his inspiration. Da Ponte and Schikaneder
succeeded in that respect with their librettos, which also have
the great advantage of being sound theatre. Beethoven's
Fidelio was not even that in its original form, and that is why

cumbersome revisions were necessary before the *Fidelio* of 1814
could emerge from the *Leonore* of 1805. The real poet, however,
was the tone poet who could turn Leonore, Florestan, Rocco,
Pizarro into those living realities which are amongst the most
precious possessions of our fantasy. But these characters live
in their music, which surrounds them like an aura—the music
which they sing. Whoever thinks of Florestan or Leonore—or
Donna Anna, or the Queen of the Night or Papageno—will
hear them sing, for their soul is their song. What applies to
Mozart's operatic personages also applies to those of Verdi:
their soul lives in their melody, just as nearly all of Verdi's
dramatic characterization is turned into melody. Even such
an extreme case of absurd melodrama as *La Forza del Destino*
can touch us, because the depth of feeling with which the
composer invests his heroes and turns it into music comes out
in every melody and every phrase whenever Leonore or Alvaro
are singing. These unhappy victims of barbaric superstitition
have become living, suffering, moving human beings. This is
genuine music which flows and throbs, even though in its form
and musical setting it is ingenuous compared with Wagner's
orchestration which is so vital and fascinating in every detail.
It is the sung melody which creates the direct contact between
the stage and the audience, and this is a valuable advantage
which can hardly be overestimated—an advantage which
Wagner's heroes only enjoy to a limited extent: in *Meistersinger*
throughout, but only occasionally in *Tristan* and the *Ring*.
Wotan speaks to us with his solemn Valhalla motif, Loge with a
flickering flame-figuration, and when we think of Siegfried we
hear his gay horn-call:

But when this horn-call appears in *Götterdämmerung*, puffed
up in strength and self-conceit, as the motif of the hero who now,
overnight, has grown up to mature manhood,

our feelings somehow refuse to accept this falsification of the happy-go-lucky lad of nature—and unfortunately our mistrust is proved right, for the inflated hero promptly falls victim to the first obvious intrigue.

Can the spontaneous expression of character which an operatic hero derives from his singing soul be replaced by a motif which is hung round his neck like a tag? I am inclined to answer this question in the negative, and it seems that Wagner in this respect did not have complete faith in his method either, for otherwise he would not have tried so desperately, by involved explanations, to furnish his heroes with a background which the traditional operatic hero can well do without. When Tamino makes his entrance in the first scene of *Zauberflöte* we are told that he is a prince, but that is all. Of Don José we only know that he is a sergeant and has a mother; anyone who wants to inform himself in more detail about his quite interesting past must read Mérimée's short story on which the *Carmen* librettists drew for their subject, but few opera goers are all that curious. Of Radames we get to know nothing except that he loves Aida, and that she is fair—and that is quite sufficient for us. But in *Tristan* half the first act is spent in telling us the early history of Tristan and Isolde, which certainly has weighty dramatic reason, but is exceedingly burdensome. And before the curtain rises for the first time in *Parsifal* so much has happened already which must be told that any listener may be forgiven if he loses patience as well as interest in what is to come. The fundamental question remains whether opera really requires all this fuss and pother. In drama it may perhaps have its place, although even there we gratefully take it as a boon that Faust tells us nothing of his past except the subjects of his studies and the negative result thereof.

The fundamental difference between a character in drama and an operatic hero is that the latter is almost completely free from intellectual presumptions. The hero in opera acts from emotional reasons, and whatever he does is above all an expression of his feelings. The conscience of Wagner the Dramatist did not allow him this liberty. True, and this is the result of his opera instinct, his heroes act just as emotionally, but there must be endless talking about it and everything must be motivated in great detail. For this reason a seam between the drama and the opera can so often be felt. His intriguers, this point has been raised earlier, are so repulsive because they are cold-blooded scoundrels without any trace of that impulsive directness with which his heroes are so generously endowed, whether it be Siegmund and Sieglinde, Tristan and Isolde, or Walter and Eva. With Wotan it is another story. It is he who has to do penance for the inconsistent construction of the *Ring*, an aimless fantastic figure, driven by dark irrational powers. All the interminable dialogues in which he gets involved cannot disguise this fact. But when he dominates the operatic stage as a hero, as in Act III of *Walküre*, he does so with incomparable aplomb.

This third act of *Walküre* is really constructed in a classical manner! First the Ride of the Valkyries; then the dramatic scene in which Sieglinde, out of deepest despair and through heroic enthusiasm, awakens to her duties of future motherhood; mighty Wotan riding in on the storm-tossed thunder clouds; the Valkyries scattering like a swarm of doves—then Brünnhilde, beginning with her *War es so schmählich* ("Was it so shameful"), leads into the uniquely beautiful final scene, the most magnificent of the opera. This scene has one perilously lengthy, somewhat sticky transition section, and anyone who knows Wagner also knows that once again he has to bridge and gloss over something. The dialogue needs an enormous amount of words to explain something which cannot be justified by *any* explanation, and occasionally the musician is compelled to get through this welter of words with musical padding of dubious validity. But then, when Wotan has made his decision—*Leb wohl, du kühnes, herrliches Kind*! (Wotan's Farewell)—the inspiration again flows in full spate, richer than ever, and the music rises in majesty and glory, from culmination to culmination, until the whole stage is filled by the blaze of the Magic Fire, and the curtain falls.

But just examine how this craftiest of all opera dramatists has hoodwinked us once again! The sleeping Brünnhilde who will one day be woken by a hero—the Sleeping Beauty behind her briars and brambles waiting for her Prince: that is one of the most imaginative inventions of myth, of fairy-tale, and that Magic Fire is the focal point and ultimate goal of the entire action of the *Ring*, whose various sections had been taken from different legendary cycles and had to be welded forcefully into a dramatic construction. All this can only be done with operatic means, all this "effect without cause". Contrition, wrath, reconciliation, exuberant love, finally a stage engulfed in a fiery blaze: that is all we really understand of the happenings in this scene, and we do not ask for more. We overlook that that brilliant magician Wagner has made us forget completely what actually *has* happened! That God, that stuffed dummy, that —— one is sorely tempted to use one of von Bülow's coarser expressions! On one single day he has had his beloved son Siegmund maliciously murdered, has consigned his beloved daughter Sieglinde to the wilderness, and has condemned his darling child Brünnhilde to exile behind a wall of flames. And now he strides off. Proudly he swings his spear, full of dignity, convinced of his divine importance and a day's work well done.

And we sit there and listen to all that without the least trace of moral indignation! Quite the contrary: we are deeply moved and feel that we have gone through an emotional upheaval, a "catharsis through fear and pity" as Aristotle once defined the effect of drama.

Now, *was* this drama?

No. It was *opera*, one of those inexplicable manifestations of Art in which our everyday concepts of good and evil, sense and non-sense, morality and immorality are no longer valid.

SELECT BIBLIOGRAPHY
LIST OF WORKS
INDEX

SELECT BIBLIOGRAPHY

Biographies

K. F. Glasenapp, *Das Leben Richard Wagners*, 1894–1911 (London, 1900–)
H. S. Chamberlain, *Richard Wagner*, 1896
J. Kapp, *Richard Wagner*, 1910
Ernest Newman, *Wagner as Man and Artist*, 1914
—*The Life of Richard Wagner*, 1933–1946
G. de Pourtalès, *Richard Wagner*, 1932
C. v. Westernhagen, *Richard Wagner, sein Werk, seine Welt*, 1956

Criticism and Aesthetics

Guido Adler, *Richard Wagner*, 1905
E. Kurth, *Romantische Harmonik und ihre Krise in Wagners "Tristan"*, 1920
A. Lorenz, *Das Geheimnis der Form bei Richard Wagner*, 1924–1933
H. Lichtenberger, *Richard Wagner, Poète et Penseur*, 1901

Letters

Richard Wagner an Mathilde Wesendonck, 1904 (London, 1905)
Briefwechsel zwischen Wagner und Liszt, 1887 (London, 1888)
Wagner an Theodor Uhlig, Wilhelm Fischer und Ferdinand Heine, 1888 (London, 1890)
Wagner an Freunde und Zeitgenossen, 1897
Wagner an Eliza Wille, 1887
Wagner an August Röckel, 1894 (London, 1897)
Wagner an seine Künstler, 1908
Wagner an Theodor Apel, 1910
Wagner an Hans von Bülow, 1910
Letters of Richard Wagner, The Burrell-Collection (New York, 1950; Frankfurt, 1953)
Wagner an Minna Wagner, 1908 (London, 1909)
The Nietzsche-Wagner Correspondence (New York, 1921)

Memoirs, Diaries, etc.

W. Weissheimer, *Erlebnisse mit Richard Wagner, Franz Liszt und vielen anderen Zeitgenossen*, 1898 (London, 1908)

P. Cornelius, *Briefe und Tagebuchblätter*, 1904

A. Neumann, *Reminiscences of Richard Wagner* (New York, 1908)

E. Michotte, *La Visite de Richard Wagner à Rossini*, 1906

F. Praeger, *Richard Wagner as I knew him*, 1892

E. Schuré, *Souvenirs sur Richard Wagner*, 1900

H. von Wolzogen, *Reminiscences of Richard Wagner* (Bayreuth, 1894)

LIST OF WORKS

I. COMPOSITIONS

Operas and Music Dramas

Die Feen, Romantic Opera (1834)

Das Liebesverbot, oder Die Novize von Palermo, Grand Comic Opera (1836)

Rienzi, der Letzte der Tribunen, Grand Opera (1840)

Der fliegende Holländer, Romantic Opera (1841)

Tannhäuser und der Sängerkrieg auf der Wartburg, Romantic Opera (1845)

Lohengrin, Romantic Opera (1848)

Der Ring des Nibelungen, ein Bühnenfestspiel (Music Drama)
    Prologue: *Das Rheingold* (1854)
        I. *Die Walküre* (1856)
        II. *Siegfried* (1871)
        III. *Götterdämmerung* (1874)

Tristan und Isolde (1859)

Die Meistersinger von Nürnberg (1867)

Parsifal, ein Bühnenweihfestspiel (1882)

Other Compositions

Overture in B flat (1830)

Piano Sonata in B flat (1832)

Piano Sonata in A (1832)

Polonaise in D for piano duet (1832)

Fantasy in F sharp minor for piano (1832)

Overture to Raupach's *König Enzio* (1832)

Concert Overture in C (1832)

Symphony in C (1832)

Overture *Polonia* (1836)

Overture *Christoph Columbus* (1836)

Overture *Rule Britannia* (1837)

Four French Romances for voice and piano (1839)
    Dors mon enfant
    Mignonne

Attente
Les deax Grenadiers
Eine Faust-Ouvertüre (1840)
Das Liebesmahl der Apostel, for men's chorus and orchestra (1843)
Album Sonata for Mathilde Wesendonck (1853)
Züricher Vielliebchen-Walzer (1853)
Fünf Gedichte von Mathilde Wesendonck (1857/8)
　Der Engel
　Träume
　Schmerzen
　Steh still
　Im Treibhaus
Albumblatt for Princess Pauline Metternich (1861)
Albumblatt (*Ankunft bei den schwarzen Schwänen*) for Countess
　Pourtalès (1861)
Albumblatt for Frau Betty Schott (1875)
Huldigungsmarsch for King Ludwig II (1865)
Siegfried-Idyll (1870)
Kaisermarsch (1871)
Grosser Festmarsch (American Centennial March) (1876)

II. Literary Works (Selection)

Eine Pilgerfahrt zu Beethoven ("Gazette Musicale") (1840)
Autobiographische Skizze (1842)
Die Kunst und die Revolution (1849)
Das Kunstwerk der Zukunft (1850)
Kunst und Klima (1850)
Das Judentum in der Musik (1850)
Oper und Drama (1851)
Ein Theater in Zürich (1851)
Eine Mitteilung an meine Freunde (1852)
Vorwort und Epilog zur Herausgabe der Dichtung von "Der Ring des
　Nibelungen" (1863)
Über Staat und Religion (1864)
Deutsche Kunst und Deutsche Politik (1868)
Über das Dirigieren (1869)
Beethoven (1870)
Mein Leben (private print) (1870)
Eine Kapitulation, Comedy in the Antique Manner (1871)
Über das Dichten und Komponieren ("Bayreuther Blätter") (1879)
Über die Anwendung der Musik auf das Drama ("Bayreuther Blätter")
　(1879)

Das Bühnenweihfestspiel in Bayreuth (1882)

Collected Works, 10 Vols. (1883)

Most of these were published in 1892–99 in eight volumes in an English translation by W. Ashton Ellis under the general title *Richard Wagner's Prose Works*.

My Life (London, 1911)

INDEX

Compiled by H. E. Crowe